THY ROD
and
THY STAFF

They Comfort Me

BOOK II

The Book of Hebrews and the Corporal Punishment of Children in the Christian Context

SAMUEL MARTIN

This volume is dedicated to the 100's of sisters and brothers in Christ who have supported me since the publication of the first edition of my book, *Thy Rod and Thy Staff, They Comfort Me: Christians and the Spanking Controversy,* published in 2006.

Cover Design and interior formatting by Dara Stoltzfus

First Edition – Fall 2019

Samuel Martin

Email: info@biblechild.com

Website: www.biblechild.com

ISBN: 978-0-9785339-4-6

The New
Foundation
for
Biblical
Research
Jerusalem

Recompense to no man evil for evil. Provide things honest in the sight of all men.

If it be possible, as much as lieth in you, live peaceably with all men.

Dearly beloved, avenge not yourselves, but rather give place unto wrath: for it is written, Vengeance is mine; I will repay, saith the Lord.

Therefore if thine enemy hunger, feed him; if he thirst, give him drink: for in so doing thou shalt heap coals of fire on his head.

Be not overcome of evil, but overcome evil with good.

--- Romans 12:17-21

TABLE OF CONTENTS

INTRODUCTION
What is the Purpose of this Book?

This book has a simple purpose. It is to give you access to more knowledge that will help you in your decision making surrounding the issue of corporal punishment of children in the Christian context. Hopefully, the knowledge that you will receive in this book will assist you further and help you to decide that corporal punishment/spanking/smacking is a practice for you as a Christian to abandon.

I want to be clear and transparent. This purpose exists because since I wrote my first book, I have received a huge amount of wonderful feedback and so many scores of people benefitted from the first book in this series. Now it is time to move to a higher level of understanding tying up the loose ends my first book left undone. The letter to the Hebrews (chapter 12:5-11) and its supposed advocacy of corporal punishment/spanking/smacking for Christians today was one subject which needed further consideration and elaboration in my first book.

The goal of my first book was to bring disparate communities of Christians who love the Word of God and people in the Children's Rights community together around the Bible so that we could all have a better understanding of this most misunderstood of Biblical teachings: spanking. The goal of this book is different. It is much more focused on Christians who continue to point to the book of Hebrews in particular saying that it advocates for Christians to spank/smack their children today.

I am grateful that my first book was well received by scholars and lay people. I have been deeply touched by so many testimonies from parents who have expressed to me how they came to understand the new truth of non-violent parenting. I have put many of these testimonies on my blog[1], on my Facebook Page[2] in addition to a number of reviews that my book received from several scholars that I posted on my website (www.biblechild.com). I continue to look forward to the good fruit that my first book continues to bear and pray that this new research study will help to strengthen the faith and security that my Christian sisters and brothers have to pursue peace and non-violence, so help us God. My first book remains free of charge.

I wish to mention finally that I think it is essential that anyone who wishes to appreciate the research in this book to please do so after having read my first book. This is essential to really understand my orientation regarding the ideas in this book.

Hebrews 12:5-11: Where do we begin?

The section of Scripture found in Hebrews 12:5-11 has been one of the most difficult texts for me to try to understand in all of the Bible. It is one that I have thought long and hard over since 2005 when I was formulating the major parts of the research for my book, *"Thy Rod and Thy Staff, They Comfort Me; Christians and the Spanking Controversy."*

This text is one that I did not address at great length in my first book. In fact, the material that I do have in my first book concerning this

---

[1] samuelmartin.blogspot.com/2013/06/twenty-two-testimonies-about-free-ebook.html
[2] www.facebook.com/byblechyld/

matter is a part of my book which I consider my weakest of the whole argument found in that book.

I really have struggled with this material. It has been so hard to engage on a number of levels. There are so many questions that need answering in my mind if we are going to ever come to some reasonable conclusions what this text means to us Christians today living in the 21st century. Thankfully, in my mind, these questions have been answered now. I am now totally at peace with the entire book of Hebrews.

This issue remains one of very serious importance. The information which speaks on the surface of disciplining children with corporal punishment found in the New Testament book of Hebrews chapter 12:5-11 is one of the most widely quoted sections of the New Testament constantly referenced by many Christian religious authorities in favor specifically of the modern teaching of spanking/smacking children.

One can find this "go to" text quoted very widely in favor of spanking/smacking children by Christian religious authorities at all levels because it seems so clear, plain and in agreement with a line of thinking elaborated by many Christians today which includes corporal punishment as the primary Biblical method for rearing children. There also exists an arrogance surrounding these interpretations of Hebrews 12:5-11 and because of this, it often makes some Christians hard to engage.

It is also used as the, "Yes, I understand what you are saying about Proverbs, but what about the Hebrews 12:5-11" argument?" by so many proponents of corporal punishment. Many will often admit that the arguments in the Old Testament might be a little weak, but that all changes because of this text in Hebrews 12:5-11. Case closed!

Many Christian parents (especially mothers), however, find this text to be a troubling one (as it is generally presented by today's well-intentioned

Christian religious authorities) because it seems, on the surface, to position the New Testament writers, who are speaking under the Holy Spirit, firmly in favor of spanking children.

Yes, this is exactly what the text, on the surface, seems to teach and this is what many Christian authorities will have us all believe (like this example[3]).

However, the question is: Does this text really teach and mean what many of our dear Christian brethren are telling us? Was this text in Hebrews relevant for some Christians, but not others? Is it enough to just open the book of Hebrews and quote this passage along with several texts in Proverbs and present your case in favor of spanking? Some say, "Yes indeed!" Not only do many spanking advocates so quickly quote this text (and this text alone) with a sense of arrogant certainty of their beliefs that any suggestion to the contrary causes the eyes to roll over and the voice of condemnation rising against anyone who suggests anything different than their view.

However, I would like to say: "Wait a minute, let's look at this matter a little bit deeper than just starting at verse five in Hebrews 12, ending at verse 11, looking at a few Greek words, quoting a few modern spanking adherents and thinking there is nothing else to say." There is a lot more to say.

Be Willing To Look Under the Surface and Find Deeper Truths
Before we look at Hebrews 12 itself, we need to step back and be willing to accept the fact that, first, the information we find in the book of Hebrews is not just meant to be a stand-alone presentation with no context. This book was written to a particular group of people at a particular time for a

---

[3] http://andynaselli.com/wp-content/uploads/2013_training.pdf

particular reason. That book had a context into which it entered and it did so in response to a particular need for it at that time.

This, however, is very much not how many Christian leaders today present this matter. They present this information as binding on all Christians today, without exception. Advocates for this view are just taking us for a visit to a certain part of Scripture which seems very much to teach what they are saying, but in doing so, they are taking us on a very limited trip *to* and *from* one text in the New Testament, but in the process they choose deliberately not to take us *in, around, through, over, under, in between, above or to try to rightly divide our trip* to understanding God's Word. (Could it be that because that rightly divided trip might lead us to another understanding and reduce the power and influence they have?). They ask few questions of the text or they will ask a few questions and then go into more detailed analyses of specific words in the text to build some kind of authoritative case for their view. Let's look at a practical comparison which might help us better capture what we are talking about.

Let's say we know someone who lives in a very conservative southern state in America. It is a beautiful state with lovely coastal climate and wonderful people. This state is in fact one of the more conservative states in America and generally follows a very family oriented, community loving, hardworking, honest approach to living.

Now is there anything wrong with this beautiful state? Is it worse than other states or better? Not necessarily. But do you think for one moment that we can extrapolate generalized opinions about "America" solely on the basis of visiting this state? Hardly anyone would agree with that idea. America is a very diverse place.

Yet, this is exactly the approach that many well intentioned Christian pastors, ministers and leaders use when it comes to this subject of spanking/smacking children and the information about this subject we find in the book of Hebrews.

I have written about the error of this approach in not only my book, "*Thy Rod and Thy Staff, They Comfort Me: Christians and the Spanking Controversy*", but I have also written about it on my blog in a number of articles. (see my blog post, *"No Biblical Text is an Island,"*-http://samuelmartin.blogspot.co.il/2014/06/no-biblical-text-is-island_19.html). The problem really with this approach is that in the end it justifies family violence as a solution to raising children and brings God and His Word into the equation as the ultimate authority for parents to undertake this practice.

Oh, how potentially dangerous and superficial this approach can be! It takes the easy road to parental control and in the process creates so much pain for little children who have to bear the brunt of this type of violent parenting undertaken in the name of Jesus Christ. Many who were raised in this way will agree with this view.

I know how this feels because I grew up in a church that took this approach to parenting and little children suffered seriously at the hands of well-intentioned (but seriously misguided and misled) parents who received inappropriate and incorrect Biblical information on this subject. For many, Hebrews 12 was quoted early and often.

This text in Hebrews was coupled with other texts in Hebrews which when used together help create a kind of "imprisonment theology". This is the cultivation of belief using Scripture which places a believer in a position of believing something which gives them no way out of the belief itself. Some Christians today feel trapped in their beliefs and Hebrews is one of the most misused Bible books in this regard today.

Many Christian interpreters of Hebrews today use corporal punishment (Heb. 12:5-11), tithing (Heb. 7:2-10), and church attendance (Heb. 10:25), to demand that Christians keep these rules. Couple these issues with the fact that in Heb. 13:17 it says:

"Obey your leaders and submit to them, for they are keeping watch over your souls..."

In fact, these teachings (as promoted today by many pastors) are presented in very superficial ways, but in a dogmatic sense, with many Christians today absolutely ordered to adhere to them or else. What is presented is the fact that many Protestant pastors tell God fearing Christian people today that they must spank their children, tithe, and attend church and if they don't do this they are in sin and come under the frightening threats given by the same pastors concerning Hebrews 6:4-6 which says:

"For it is impossible for those who were once enlightened, and have tasted of the heavenly gift, and were made partakers of the Holy Ghost, And have tasted the good word of God, and the powers of the world to come, If they shall fall away, to renew them again unto repentance; seeing they crucify to themselves the Son of God afresh, and put him to an open shame." (ESV)

This is a major text used to threaten Christians that if they do not listen and heed the words of this book as interpreted by many misguided pastors, they are going fall under the curses listed herein and will be placed in the category of "**impossible ... to renew them again unto repentance.**" One can see the "imprisonment" nature of the theology. It is terrifying. Coupling these texts together can create this horrible cocktail of fear. But does this need to be so? Is this really what Hebrews is teaching?

When we put all of these four teachings together as often presented by many well intentioned (but seriously misguided) pastors/religious leaders, you have a poisonous theological cocktail which is presented in a way that imprisons the souls of dear Christian people and helps put them a kind of spiritual prison with no escape.

Let's Step Back and Take a Bigger Picture View of This Question

Now, we have to step back and take a bigger picture view of the book of Hebrews because it is found in the New Testament for a reason. To understand what that reason is, we have to have some deeper background information on not only the book of Hebrews, but also on the whole of the New Testament itself. We will start with this question of New Testament design after which we will examine the matters of who wrote Hebrews, why the author did not openly identify himself, when it was written and to where it was directed geographically. This will be the foundation for our study.

It is essential that we abandon this superficial examination of the Biblical texts and start to look more deeply at the entire body of Scripture. To think that we are going to understand a single text or the ideas it presents outside of its wider context within the individual book or within the various collections of books written by the same author or as those books relate one to another is a mistaken notion. Bible teachings must be compatible with a good systematic theology which is established using solid principles of Bible interpretation. Methodologies which lead to this "imprisonment theology" which uses violence to achieve their aims and creates mechanisms of control over people must be called into question and challenged. That is what we are doing in this book calling believers to rethink the book of Hebrews and its relevance and application today.

TIMELINE

Since we are going to be discussing history dealing with facts about people and places, it is also helpful for us to property orient ourselves from a calendrical point of view. When things happened is quite important for our discussion here, so I am going to give a brief general outline first to assist our framing of the relevant dates for our consideration. Let us consider a general chronological outline of some general events of the New Testament which can help us see the overall period we are concerned with.

Note that the second and third dates listed below are based on my late father's research dealing with the birth of Jesus in several books he wrote on that subject.

Paul Born .... 5 BC

Jesus Born .... 3 BC

Herod Died (This date is noted in J. Finegan following D. Beyer) .... 1 BC

Jesus visits the Temple as a 12 year old .... 10 AD

Christ's First Year of Teaching .... 27-28 AD

Sabbatical Year in the First Century among the Jewish people .... 27-28 AD

First Passover mentioned in John's Gospel (6:4) .... 29 AD

Feast of Tabernacles mentioned in John's Gospel (7:1) .... 29 AD

Feast of the Dedication mentioned in John's Gospel (10:22) .... 29/30AD(winter)

Jesus Crucified, Buried and Raised from the Dead .... 30 AD (Passover)

17

18

[4] This proposed chronological reconstruction comes from a paper by late father, Dr. Ernest L. Martin, titled: *"The Year of Christ's Crucifixion."* (Foundation for Biblical Research, Pasadena: CA, April 1983)

1

The original manuscript order of Hebrews and its importance?

It may seem a little strange to start out this discussion of seeking a deeper understanding of Hebrews 12:5-11 (and how Christian advocates of spanking/smacking children use this text to prove that the New Testament teaches Christian parents of the necessity to spank/smack their children) with a seemingly unconnected issue related to New Testament Textual Criticism,[5] but I start at this point by necessity. This is because today, in our modern world, our New Testament, which we all know and love, has been presented to us in a dress which does not reflect the best evidence as found in the hard science of New Testament Textual Criticism and when we study this matter, we can see how it affects even how we think, feel or even what we believe about a particular book or a particular collection of New Testament books.

This may seem strange and almost impossible to believe, but it is a simple fact and one which I believe is not only important to the issue of developing an accurate understanding of Hebrews 12:5-11, but also a

---

[5] "The textual criticism of the New Testament is the analysis of the manuscripts of the New Testament, whose goals include identification of transcription errors, analysis of versions, and attempts to reconstruct the original."
https://en.wikipedia.org/wiki/Textual_criticism_of_the_New_Testament

realization that to really understand the teachings of the New Testament, one needs to engage in a much deeper and a more comprehensive study. This approach to study must, in my view, take a much larger overview of not only the individual texts like Hebrews 12:5-11, but how those texts relate to the other material in the book of Hebrews, how Hebrews relates to other books in the collection of St. Paul's writings, how St. Paul's writings relate not only to each other, but to other collections of writings in the New Testament including the Gospels and Acts and the General Epistles (James, I & II Peter, I,II,III John and Jude). To do this, however, we first have to start with a New Testament standard which is reflected in the best manuscript evidentiary sources we have available today.

Let us be clear what we are talking about. It is simply this. Today, almost all published New Testament versions, no matter in what language they are produced, follow a design and order of books which does not reflect the best evidence we have from the large body of New Testament manuscript evidence that we have available.

Here, thankfully, we are not speaking about the translations of the texts themselves. Many fine and high quality academic translations exist and provide the Christian with accurate translations of the Greek original. However, this is not what we are talking about. What we are talking about is not how the words are translated, but rather how the entire New Testament is designed and how the material is presented and in what order. Let us look at this issue in a practical way to help us appreciate its importance. Here my late father lays out the importance of this issue of the order and positioning of the Biblical books in his book *"Restoring the Original Bible."*

"Suppose you bought a novel containing 49 chapters which introduced the various characters and plot in a progressive way from start to finish. Would it not be difficult to understand what the plot was all about if, in the first 22 chapters, chapter 16 followed immediately after chapter 6, and especially if the chapters were not properly numbered? What then if chapter 22 were placed after chapter 7, chapter 22 before 21, chapter 14 after 21, chapters 12 and 13 followed 14, chapter 18 positioned after 13, chapter 17 followed 8 and 9, chapter 20 after 10, and finally chapter 11 came after chapter 20? This would represent utter confusion. But if one reckons the chapters of our hypothetical novel as being the books of the Old Testament, this is the exact sequence we are saddled with in our present Bibles.

Let's not stop with the Old Testament. Look at what has happened when we add the 27 New Testament books. Return once more to the illustration of our novel. It means that chapters 23 to 27 follow immediately after chapter 11. Chapters 28 to 34 are found after chapter 44, while chapter 44 itself follows chapter 48, and chapters 35 to 43 are positioned after chapter 27. This is further confusion.

Some might say, however, that a comparison of the Bible with a novel is not proper. But this is exactly where the first mistake is made in appreciating the manuscript order of the biblical documents. It will be shown in this book that there is a definite weaving together of a single story theme through the biblical books. And it is a remarkably consistent account which often amazes people when they see it for the first time. The only reason that such a homogeneous narrative has not been recognized by most people today is because none of our published Bibles has the books of the Old and New Testaments in the original manuscript order. When the proper design is restored, a marvelous and revealing series of connected subjects is seen running through the Bible which illustrates a compatible and coherent account from beginning to end. ... This information may well prove to be an eye-opener to many students of the Bible—facts that have never been realized before."[6]

Let us also be clear that we are here not talking about some fringe idea. This idea has been known and accepted as fact by competent New Testament scholars for more than a century and a half! The main reason that they have not fixed this error is economic because it would present the New Testament in a way which would be unfamiliar to Christians today and create too many questions and may affect Bible sales.

In the above quotation, the book of Hebrews is referenced as "chapter 44" and in all English Bibles today, Hebrews comes at the end of St. Paul's collection of epistles. But, in ancient times and in the vast majority of ancient manuscripts, this wasn't the correct order of the Biblical books. Let us note the following visual representation taken from "*The New Testament in the Original Greek*"[7] that demonstrates the true order of St. Paul's epistles in particular.

What is interesting about the following graphic is that one does not really even need to read Greek to see what we are here talking about. The book of Hebrews is found in the tenth position between II Thessalonians and before I Timothy.

---

[6] Martin, Ernest L. *Restoring the Original Bible*: Ask Publications; Portland: OR, 1994. p.2
[7] Westcott, Brooke Foss and Hort, Fenton John Anthony, *The New Testament in the Original Greek*: The MacMillan Company; New York: NY, 1948. p.350

ΠΡΟΣ ΡΩΜΑΙΟΥΣ

ΠΡΟΣ ΚΟΡΙΝΘΙΟΥΣ Α

ΠΡΟΣ ΚΟΡΙΝΘΙΟΥΣ Β

ΠΡΟΣ ΓΑΛΑΤΑΣ

ΠΡΟΣ ΕΦΕΣΙΟΥΣ

ΠΡΟΣ ΦΙΛΙΠΠΗΣΙΟΥΣ

ΠΡΟΣ ΚΟΛΑΣΣΑΕΙΣ

ΠΡΟΣ ΘΕΣΣΑΛΟΝΙΚΕΙΣ Α

ΠΡΟΣ ΘΕΣΣΑΛΟΝΙΚΕΙΣ Β

ΠΡΟΣ ΕΒΡΑΙΟΥΣ

ΠΡΟΣ ΤΙΜΟΘΕΟΝ Α

ΠΡΟΣ ΤΙΜΟΘΕΟΝ Β

ΠΡΟΣ ΤΙΤΟΝ

ΠΡΟΣ ΦΙΛΗΜΟΝΑ

This figure is of the page in the Greek New Testament of Westcott and Hort[8] (1881) showing the order of St. Paul's epistles in the vast majority of Greek manuscripts available of the New Testament. The book of Hebrews appears in the tenth position in the list.

This is the exact position (the tenth letter among a collection of 14 letters of St. Paul) that we find the book of Hebrews occupying in the largest body of available New Testament manuscripts. This is the precise testimony of competent authorities who are experts on the criticism of the New Testament manuscripts. Note the explicit statement of Professor Caspar

---

[8] Westcott, B.F & Hort, F.J.A: *The New Testament in Greek*, Macmillan Co. New York, 1948.

Rene Gregory, an eminent New Testament scholar who lived about 100 years ago, who said:

"The order in which we place the books of the New Testament is not a matter of indifference. Every Christian should be familiar with these books, and should know precisely where to find each book. Every New Testament should have the books in precisely the same order, the order of the Greek Church, which in this case is of right the guardian of this ancient literature [see Romans 3:1,2]. The proper order is, I think:
First, the Four Gospels: Matthew, Mark, Luke, and John. Second, the Book of Acts. Third, the Catholic Epistles: James, First and Second Peter, First, Second, and Third John, and Jude. Fourth, the Epistles of Paul: Romans, First and Second Corinthians, Galatians, Ephesians, Philippians, Colossians, First and Second Thessalonians, Hebrews, First and Second Timothy, Titus, Philemon. And fifth, the Book of Revelation ... The Greek order is that which places the Epistle to the Hebrews between Thessalonians and Timothy, and that is the order to which we should hold. The Latin order [of Jerome] places Hebrews after Philemon. But we must keep to the old order or we shall have the New Testament turned upside down in connection with every fancied discovery as to authorship and date of books."[9]

Professor Gregory is right. Every Christian should know that the order of the New Testament books mentioned by him is the order which is reflected in the vast majority of ancient manuscripts and it is the one we should use and adhere to today.

---

[9] Gregory, Caspar Rene, *Canon and Text of the New Testament,* Charles Scribner's Sons: NY, 1907.   pp.467–469, (words in brackets are mine)

The Importance of the order of the books of the New Testament And how this helps us understand the book of Hebrews and its teachings better

Now that we have properly oriented ourselves as to the proper position of the book of Hebrews among St. Paul's letters in the New Testament collection overall, now we can consider why this is important. The reason for this is that Hebrews as a book is fundamentally different than any other book in the Pauline collection.[10] Because of this, it was positioned in the place in the collection of St. Paul's letters where it is.

One can notice the introduction to the book of Hebrews compared to all of the other 13 books in St. Paul's collection. It is fundamentally different in how it begins. Hebrews just begins with the message of the book with no mention of God, our Lord Jesus, the Holy Spirit, no specific salutation, no author identification, no identification of co-authors, no community, no church, it just seemingly starts off immediately into the main discussion of the book.

However, this is only part of the issue. We really need to dig deep into trying to understand Hebrews in its overall context. In this regard, I believe that my late father, Dr. Ernest Martin, presented some very important and compelling ideas in this regard. In his book, *Restoring the Original Bible*, he had an excellent section dealing with the whole issue of the Pauline Epistles and why their positioning and arrangement is important. This is also essential to understand the message of the book of Hebrews. This is a long section and I am going to add comments to it to help

---

[10] I will not be engaging in any consideration of the idea that St. Paul was not overall responsible for the book of Hebrews. It appears in the midst of his collection and while he may have had other people involved in its composition, fundamentally it was produced under his guidance. We will be reviewing the evidence for Pauline authorship of Hebrews later in this book.

contextualize it to our discussion here. This section is found in chapter 23 titled "The Epistles of Paul" of the previously mentioned book. He begins with a short reiteration of the importance of placing Hebrews after II Thessalonians and before I Timothy saying:

"The proper positioning of the Book of Hebrews in the manuscripts is right after Second Thessalonians just before First Timothy. Nearly all the best manuscript evidence supports this. Scrivener writes:
"In the Pauline epistles, that to the Hebrews immediately follows the second to the Thessalonians in the four great codices Vaticanus, Sinaiticus, Alexandrinus, and Ephraemi." (Introduction, vol. I, p.74)

In the margin of his work, Prof. Scrivener lists some of the many manuscripts which position the Book of Hebrews in this fashion. The evidence for this arrangement is so strong that one wonders why Hebrews was moved out of its manuscript order and placed at the back of Paul's works? The reason is not difficult to discover. Scrivener mentions a major purpose why the Western Church relegated Hebrews to last position. It was "an arrangement which at first, no doubt, originated in the early scruples prevailing in the Western Church, with respect to the authorship and canonical authority of that divine epistle." The Western Churchmen often did not believe Paul wrote Hebrews.

The Latin section of the church found it difficult to believe that the epistle was from the pen of Paul and because of this many refused to accept it as belonging in the New Testament. Most easterners had no major reservations about the book. Jerome, the great western scholar and translator of the Latin Vulgate version (a translation from the Hebrew and Greek into the Latin language), shows the differences of opinions among

27

the eastern and western sections of the church regarding the Book of Hebrews.

In his letter to Dardanus, Jerome wrote:

"To our own people [Christians], we must say that this Epistle, which is inscribed To the Hebrews,' is received as the Apostle Paul's, not only in the churches of the east, but by all the ecclesiastical writers of former times. But the Latins do not receive it among the canonical scriptures." (Whytehead, A Handbook to the Canon and Inspiration to the Scriptures, p.131)" (Martin, *Restoring the Original Bible*, pg. 358-9)

Martin continues mentioning the prevailing view among Western Churchmen why they rejected the Pauline authorship of Hebrews:
"There was a belief that Paul, the apostle to the Gentiles, had no reason to be writing to the Jews. This, of course, is not a proper evaluation. When the apostle Paul was commissioned by Christ on the road to Damascus, he was told to teach to Israelites as well as Gentiles (Acts 9:15), and throughout the history of Paul's ministry he always went to the Jews first. Indeed, he understood that it was absolutely essential to do this. Paul said: "It was necessary that the word of God should first have been spoken to you [the Jews]" (Acts 13:46). Paul's motto was: "The Jew first, and also the Greek (Gentile)" (Romans 1:16).[11]

What we need to do is to get back to a more original unbiased view which places the book of Hebrews after II Thessalonians and before I Timothy. Note also the following:

---

[11] Martin, E. *Restoring the Original Bible*: Ask Publications; Portland: OR, 1994. p.360

Further evidence from the excellent Newberry Study Bible.[12] This is a list of all of the manuscripts consulted in the preparation of that Bible. One can note in the list how Newberry followed. In his list, he notes: Gospels; of the Acts and General Epistles; of St. Paul's Epistles.

How did Hebrews get into our modern English Versions
in its present order?

This is an important question. Here the evaluation of Dr. Bullinger is very important:

"Our English Bibles follow the order as given in the Latin Vulgate. This order, therefore, depends on the arbitrary judgment of one man, Jerome

---

[12] Newberry, Thomas: *The Newberry Bible*, Hodder and Stoughton, London: 1906, pgs. xx-xxi

(A.D. 382-429) All theories based on this order rest on human authority, and are thus without any true foundation."[13]

The order of our books today comes from this Latin version of the Bible produced by St. Jerome. It is here where the error began, but today we have the evidence to see through this error and undo this damage.

What we are going to see are things about the New Testament and its teachings and design which we have never seen before and what we can learn can transform our understanding of this book of Hebrews.

To conclude, in this research study, we will focus on St. Paul's book of Hebrews in the tenth position among his other letters, which are 14 in number total. Starting out with the proper orientation and positioning of the book of Hebrews will hopefully help us in better understanding the book as a whole.

---

[13] Bullinger, Dr. E. W., The Companion Bible, Lamp Press: London, Appendix 95, pg. 139

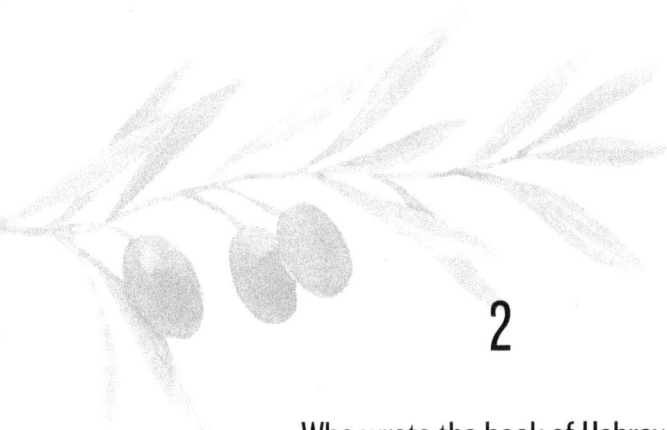

2

Who wrote the book of Hebrews?

As we have seen in the previous chapter, the book of Hebrews appears as the tenth in a collection of texts ascribed generally to St. Paul. Certainly, there are other co-authors of some of Paul's letters (this will be discussed later), but overall we identify them with St. Paul. It is the view of this author as a key understanding of this book that the book of Hebrews was written by St. Paul. (If not directly certainly under his direction, authority, and guidance)

This assertion is attested by an overwhelming number of ancient authorities. I am mentioning this here because there is a strong tendency among modern scholars to say that Paul did not write Hebrews for a variety of reasons. (See Appendix II) I think it reasonable to quote Nathaniel Lardner here whose review of the ancient authorities who affirmed that Paul wrote Hebrews is in my view quite convincing. I think this detailed quotation will provide some excellent and compelling evidence for our assertion here of the Pauline authorship of Hebrews.

Lardner says the following in this very rich quote:

"I now proceed to the third inquiry, who is the writer of this epistle [Hebrews]. And many things offer in favour of the apostle Paul.

1. It is ascribed to him by many of the ancients.

Here I think myself obliged briefly to recollect the testimonies of ancient authors, which have been produced at large in the preceding volumes. And I shall rank them under two heads: first, the testimonies of writers who used the Greek tongue, then the testimonies of those who lived in that part of the Roman Empire, where the Latin was the vulgar language.

There are some passages in the epistle of Ignatius about the year 107, which may be thought by some to contain allusions to the epistle of the Hebrews. The epistle seems to be referred to by Polycarp bishop of Smyrna, in his epistle written to the Philippians in the year 108, and in the relation of his martyrdom, written about the middle of the second century. This epistle is often quoted as Paul's by Clement of Alexandria, about the year 194. It is received, and quoted as Paul's by Origen, about 230. It was also received as the apostle's by Dionysius, bishop of Alexandria in 247. It is plainly referred to by Theognostus of Alexandria, about 282, by Pamphilus, about 294, and by Archelaus, bishop in Mesopotamia, at the beginning of the fourth century, by the Manichees in the fourth, and by the Paulicians, in the seventh century. It was received, and ascribed to Paul by Alexander, bishop of Alexandria, in the year 313, and by the Arians in the fourth century. Eusebius, bishop of Caesarea, about 315, says, 'There are fourteen epistles of Paul, manifest and well known; but yet there are some, who reject that to the Hebrews, alleging, in behalf of their opinion, that it was not received by the church of Rome, as a writing of Paul.' It is often quoted by Eusebius himself, as Paul's, and sacred scripture. This epistle was received by Athanasius without any hesitation. In his enumeration of St. Paul's fourteen epistles, this is placed next after the two to the

Thessalonians, and before the epistles to Timothy, Titus, and Philemon. The same order is observed in the Synopsis of scripture ascribed to him. This epistle is received as Paul's by Adamantius, author of a dialogue against the Marcionites in 330, and by Cyril of Jerusalem, in 348, by the council of Laodicea, in 363. Where St. Paul's epistles are enumerated in the same order, as in Athanasius, just taken notice of. This epistle is also received as Paul's by Epiphanius, about 368, by the Apostolic Constitutions, about the end of the fourth century, by Basil, about 370, by Gregory Nazianzen, in 370, by Amphilochius also. But he says it was not received by all as Paul's. It was received by Gregory Nyssen, about 371, by Didymus of Alexandria, about the same time, by Ephrem the Syrian, in 370, and by the church of Syria, by Diodorus of Tarsus, in 378, by Hierax, a learned Egyptian, about the year 302, by Serapion, bishop of Thmuis in Egypt, about 347, by Titus, bishop of Bostra, in Arabia, about 362, by Theodore, bishop of Mopsuestia, in Cilicia, about the year 394, by Chrysostom, at the year 398, by Severian, bishop of Gabala, in Syria, 401, by Victor of Antioch, about 401, by Palladius, author of a life of Chrysostom, about 408, by Isidore of Pelusium, about 412, by Cyril, bishop of Alexandria, in 412, by Theodoret, at 423, by Eutherius, bishop of Tyana, in Cappadocia, in 431, by Socrates, the Ecclesiastical Historian, about 440, by Euthalius, in Egypt, about 458, and, probably, by Dionysius, falsely called the Areopagite; by the author of the Questiones et Responsiones, commonly ascribed to Justin Martyr, but rather written in the fifth century. It is in the Alexandrian manuscript, about the year 500, and in the Stoichometry of Nicephorus, about 806, is received as Paul's by Cosmas of Alexandria, about 535, by Leontius, of Constntinople, about 610, by John Damascen, in 730, by Photius, about 858, by Oecumenius, about the 950, and by Theophylact in 1070. I shall not go any lower.

I shall now rehearse such authors as lived in that part of the Roman Empire, where the Latin was the vulgar tongue.

Here in the first place offers Clement in his epistle to the Corinthians, written about the year 96, or, as some others say, about the year 70, For though he wrote in Greek, we rank him among Latin authors, because he was bishop of Rome. In his epistle are divers passages, generally supposed to contain allusions, or references to the epistle to the Hebrews. Irenaeus, bishop of Lyons, about 178, as we are assured by Eusebius, alleged some passages out of this epistle, in a work now lost. Nevertheless, it does not appear, that he received it as St. Paul's. ... It was received as Paul's by Hilary of Poietiers, about 354, and by Lucifer, bishop of Cagliari, in Sardinia, about the same time, and by his followers. It was also received as Paul's by C.M. Victorinus. ... It was received as Paul's by Ambrose, bishop of Milan, about 374, by the Priscillianists, about 378. ... It was received as Paul's by Philaster, bishop of Brescia in Italy, about 380. ... His successor quotes this epistle as Paul's. It is also readily received as Paul's by Jerome, about 392. And he says, it was generally received by the Greeks, and the Christians in the east, ... It was received as Paul's by Rufinus in 397. It is also in the catalogue of the third council of Carthage in 397. It is frequently quoted by Augustin as St. Paul's. ... But he [Augustin] was included to follow the opinion of the churches in the east, who received it among the canonical scriptures. It was received as Paul's by Chromatius, bishop of Aquileia, in Italy about 401, by Innocent, bishop of Rome, about 402, by Paulinus, bishop of Nola, in Italy, in 403. ... It was received by Cassian, about 424, by Propser of Aquitain, about 434, and by the authors of the words ascribed to him; by Eucherius, bishop of Lyon, in 434, by Sedulius, about 818, by Leo, bishop of Rome, in 440, Salvian, presbyter of Marseilles, about 440, by Gelasius, bishop of Rome, about 496, by

Facundus, an African bishop, about 540, by Junilius, an African bishop, about 556, by Cassiodorius, in 556, by the author of the imperfect Work upon St. Matthew, about 560, by Gregory, bishop of Rome, about 590, by Isidore of Seville, about 596, and by Bede, about 701."[14]

Not every authority quoted by Lardner agrees that it comes from the inspired pen of St. Paul. However, the vast majority of the major Church fathers hold that it was authored by St. Paul, especially those authorities who originated in the eastern part of the Church. On the basis of these numerous witnesses, in this work, we will be taking the view that St. Paul is the author of Hebrews or that the publication came together under his complete guidance and supervision and that it rightly must be included in a collection of his 14 letters to be found after II Thessalonians and before I Timothy.

---

[14] *ibid.* pgs.88-91

3

If St. Paul authored Hebrews, why did he not identify himself?

Hebrews is a very different composition than any of Paul's other writings. Paul is nowhere identified by name in the book. This is very different than all of Paul's other writings which start out with his first name as well as mentioning others who also participated in his letter writing activities (like **Sosthenes** – I Cor. 1:1; **Timothy** – Phil. 2:19; I Cor. 4:17ff; 16:10,11; **Silas** – I Thess. 1:1; II Thess. 1:1).

In addition, at the end of Romans, I Corinthians, Colossians, II Timothy, Titus and Philemon all have a number of persons mentioned at the end of the texts, but Hebrews gives one small mention of Timothy only.

Hebrews is fundamentally a different type of work compared to the other New Testament letters and this is apparent to anyone who looks at the book in an objective way. Let us consider why Paul did not include his name to this book.

Biblical commentators have been discussing this issue for hundreds of years offering many different views as to why Paul did not add his own name. In this regard, we can again refer to Lardner here whose testimony is indispensable saying:

"3. Obj. There still remains one objection more against this epistle being written by St. Paul: which is the want of his name. For all the thirteen epistles, received as his, he prefixeth his name, and generally calleth himself apostle.

This objection had been obvious in all ages. And the omission has been differently accounted for by the ancients, who received this epistle as a genuine writing of St. Paul.

Clement of Alexandria, in his institutions, as cited by us formerly from Eusebius, speaks to this purpose, The epistle to the Hebrews, he says, is Paul's. But he did not make use of that inscription, 'Paul the apostle.' Of which he assigns this reason. Writing to the Hebrews, who had conceived a prejudice against him, and were suspicious of him, he wisely declined setting his name at the beginning, lest he should offend them. He also mentions this tradition: forasmuch as the Lord was sent as the apostle of Almighty God to the Hebrews, Paul out of modesty does not style himself the apostle of the Hebrews; both out of respect to the Lord, and that being preacher and apostle of the Gentiles, he over and above wrote to the Hebrews.

Jerome also speaks to this purpose, 'That Paul might decline putting his name in the inscription, on account of the Hebrews being offended with him.' So in the article of St. Paul, in his book of Illustrious Men. In his commentary upon the beginning of the epistle to the Galatians, he assigns another reason, that Paul declined to style himself apostle at the beginning of the epistle to the Hebrews, because he should afterwards call Christ the high priest, and apostle of our profession.' See Ch. iii, 1.

Theodoret says, that Paul was especially the apostle of the Gentiles. For which he allegeth, Gal. ii.9, and Rom. xi.13. 'Therefore writing to the Hebrews, who were not entrusted to his care, **he barely delivered the doctrine of the gospel**, without assuming any character of authority. For they were the charge of the other apostles." (Lardner, *Credibility*, vol. vi. Pgs. 107-108)

Lardner features some additional comments about this issue which are very relevant for our consideration here saying:

"Lighfoot says, 'Paul's not affixing his name to this, as he had done to his other epistles, does no more deny it to be his, than the first epistle of John is denied to be John's upon that account.'

Tillemont says, 'Possibly Paul considered it as a book, rather than a letter; since he makes an excuse for its brevity, ch.xiii.22. For indeed it is short for a book, but long for a letter.' The same thought is in Estius. This may induce us to recollect an observation of Chrysostom to the like purpose, formerly taken notice of.

It is, I think observable, that there is not at the beginning of this epistle any salutation. As there is no name of the writer, so neither is there any description of the people, to whom it is sent. It appears from the conclusion, that is was sent to some people in a certain place. And, undoubtedly, they to whom it was sent, and by whom it was received, knew very well from whom it came. Nevertheless there might be reasons for omitting an inscription, and a salutation at the beginning. This might arise from the circumstances of things. There might be danger of offence in sending at that time a long letter to Jews in Judea. And this omission might be in part owing to a regard for the bearer, who too is not named. The only person named throughout the epistle is Timothy. Nor was he at that time present with the writer.

Indeed, I imagine, that the two great objections against this being a genuine epistle of the apostle; the elegance of the style, and the want of a name and inscription, are both owing to some particular circumstances of the writer, and the people to whom it was sent. The people, to whom it was sent are plainly Jews in Judea; and the writer, very probably, is Paul. Whose circumstances at the breaking up of his confinement at Rome, and his setting out upon a new journey, might be attended with some peculiar embarrassments; which obliged him to act differently from his usual method." (*ibid.* pg. 109)

Chrysostom gives us some very important suggestions to consider. The circumstances of the people and the sender of the book of Hebrews were definitely facing a difficult situation when the letter was sent to them.

We know that Paul was imprisoned many times (seven times said Clement in his Epistle to the Corinthians). As time went on, the situation got so difficult that Paul eventually was executed. It is very possible that due to the situation taking place in the Roman Empire near the time Paul died in the run up to the Jewish/Roman War in 70 AD, the political environment was much more difficult and questions of seeing one's writings preserved were front and center in the mind of St. Paul.

We can also add to this the very interesting and relevant testimony of Dr. Bullinger, who we will refer to at length later in this book. He said the following, which we should pay close attention to:

"It was written by Paul, as is clear from a comparison of I Peter 1:1; II Peter 3:1,15. But his name is omitted, so that Jews might not be prejudiced against its teaching and **that the churches might not confuse it with other Pauline Epistles addressed to them.**"[15]

---

[15] Bullinger, E. W., *Things to Come*, Vol. VII, No. 8. Pg. 99 – Art. "The Epistle to the Hebrews"

This is a very instructive comment by Dr. Bullinger which will be of some importance later in our discussion. This is because in all of Paul's letters to the seven Churches he wrote to, he identified himself openly and clearly, whereas in the letter to the Hebrews, he did not. Non-Hebrew Christian readers would have noted right away the differences between other letters they had seen from St. Paul coupled with the fact that the material found in the book of Hebrews is very much focused on the law-keeping Hebrew Christian believers living in the land of Israel in a Temple oriented society.

We also have to consider the fact that Hebrews may contain information in it which Paul is trying very much to communicate to the Jewish Christians in Judea before the war with a particular focus on urging them to realize that Jesus was not returning from heaven as soon as Paul and others had previously thought. This was based even on what the Lord Jesus had said (Matt. 16:28) and that there was going to be many more years in advance of them and that they should no longer think that Jesus was returning to Earth in their lifetimes. Paul may have wanted to relay this information in a more indirect way for those who "had eyes to see, and ears to hear."

Trying to keep the meaning hidden – Biblical Examples to Consider
We all know that our Lord Jesus used parables in His teaching methods (Matthew 13:34) and those parables often were not easy to understand. Even His disciples asked Him to explain His parabolic teachings to them (Matthew 13:36). It is clear in Scripture that we have examples where books are sealed or have teachings in them which may be hidden or secret. (Deuteronomy 29:29) Our Lord Jesus said many times: "He who has ears to hear, let him hear." (Matthew 11:15; 13:9; Mark 4:23; Revelation 3:13) To

understand what He was teaching, one had to be spiritually in tune with His message. Not only that, we know that Jesus did not reveal all of His teachings even to His own disciples. They were simply not ready to receive them at that time. "I have yet many things to say unto you, but ye cannot bear them now" (John 16:12 KJV).

We also need to understand that circumstances that some people in the Biblical period found themselves in, caused them to use certain techniques to hide their teachings. In effect, what they were doing was giving the truth, but it was a truth to those who were initiated. Several good examples of this are found in the book of Jeremiah. It is often not understood, but certain pieces of information in the Bible were given to those who were initiated into the teachings being given at that time. Those teachings were hidden for different reasons. Look at Jeremiah 25:26 and 51:41:

"and all the kings of the north, near and far, one with another; and all the kingdoms of the earth which are upon the face of the ground, and the king of **Sheshach** shall drink after them." (25:26)

"How **Sheshak** has been captured, And the praise of the whole earth been seized!" (51:41)

Anyone can review any of the online Bibles or commentaries about these two verses and all of them will say that the words above in bold are backward ciphers for the word "Babylon." We do not know exactly why Jeremiah uses this literary device because in other verses in his book, he uses the word "Babylon." (24:1; 25:1) However, scholars recognize that these words (Shechach/Sheshak) mean "Babylon" and a technique known

41

as "*atbash*" is being employed. This means that in the Hebrew alphabet, the first letter becomes the last letter and the second letter becomes the next to the last letter and so on through the entire alphabet.

There is another instance of this technique used by Jeremiah in 51:1 saying:

"Thus says the Lord: "Behold, I will stir up the spirit of a destroyer against Babylon, against the inhabitants of Leb-kamai."

This phrase "*Leb-kamai*" is also an "atbash" and it means not "Babylon", but it means the "Chaldeans". (לבקמי ← כשדים) This is well known among Bible scholars.

Keil and Delitsch mention their viewpoint of this verse in Jeremiah 51:1 saying:

"In li.1-4, the terrible character of the hostile nations is further described. Against Babylon and the inhabitants of Chaldea, God stirs up the 'spirit of a destroyer,' viz. a savage nation that will massacre the Chaldeans without pity. לב קמי (Hebrew: *Leb-kamai*), lit. 'the heart of mine adversaries,' is the word כשדים (Hebrew: Chaldeans), changed, according to the canon Atbash (see xxv.26), for the purpose of obtaining the important meaning that Chaldea is the centre of God's enemies. This explanation of the name involves the thought that all enmity against God the Lord culminates in Babylon;" (Keil and Delitzsch, Commentary on Jeremiah, pg. 289)

We are not 100% certain why this technique is used, but Jeremiah and certain of his readers knew what he meant. It definitely has a meaning

42

and this meaning is not to be understood unless God reveals it to us. Clearly, there is a meaning here which is hidden using this Atbash literary device.

It has also been suggested by some scholars that St. Peter in I Peter 5:13 where he mentions "Babylon" may very well be referring to Jerusalem but uses another geographical place name because he did not wish to refer to Jerusalem then openly.

Numerical devices found in Scripture

Sometimes not only are words used, but sometimes numerical features are also used.

The Bible is full of numerical relationships. For example, note the following verse from the book of Psalms:

"I have set the Lord always before me: Surely he is at my right hand, I shall not be moved" - Psalm 16:8

This passage is one that I want to bring to your attention from the inspired pen of David in this numerical context. There are many important aspects to this verse, but I wanted only to talk about one.

The book of Psalms is a very special book with lots of complexities and it is one that we need to look at closely and carefully because it is full of information if we are just willing to see it.

God gave the writers of Psalms inspiration and it comes out in many ways. Some of the important things that many have seen in Psalms are the various literary devices that are used to convey ideas and in some cases, we can note the numerical nature of these literary devices.

For example, many of us may be familiar with the literary device called acrostics. It is the idea that there are these 22 verse segments where each letter of the Hebrew alphabet begins the first word of the particular section. Psalm 119 is the prime example of several found in the Bible. They indicate a kind of literary completeness or perfection. We also have broken acrostics (where some of the letters in the series are missing) that show a sense of evil or incompleteness like Psalms 9-10.

We also find that there are other numerical features that are very interesting in the Psalms whose meanings we are still trying to understand better.

One of them is found in this verse I have given here, Psalm 16:8. The first things about this verse right away is an association with the number 8. Note Psalm 16 and verse 8. This is not the only association with the number 8 for this verse.

In the original Hebrew, there are 32 letters to this verse. They are:

שויתי יהוה לנגדי תמיד כי מימיני בל אמוט

It is really interesting to see these relationships used with numbers because they have meaning; it is just there for us to find out the truth.

Note that this verse, written by David, has a three-fold relationship with the number eight to it being the 8th verse, of the 16th chapter with 32 letters. There are many similar things with number in Scripture, which we don't need to go into now. However, note that we know that the number 888 is associated with Jesus Christ.

This is something I learned a long time ago about the name of Jesus. It has a numerical value that is quite remarkable. The name "Jesus" in English comes from the Greek name Ιησους (*Iesous*). In the Greek language, each of the letters possesses a numerical value. Here are the numerical values for Ιησους:

I - 10
η - 8
σ - 200
ο - 70
υ - 400
ζ - 200

Total – 888

Interesting numerical relationships are found in other passages of Scripture. For example, in Daniel 3:1 we read:

"King Nebuchadnezzar made an image of gold, whose height was sixty cubits and its breadth six cubits. He set it up on the plain of Dura, in the province of Babylon."

This text has a very interesting numerical relationship whose meaning is not 100% clear, but is in evidence for all to see.

This was referenced in a work by my late father discussing this text saying:

"This king Nebuchadnezzar was the Babylonian head of gold who was to dominate all political and religious power in the earth until the Kingdom of God would be set up under Israel's Messiah. Note that the image set up by Nebuchadnezzar was crafted around measurements of 6. But that does not end the matter. Dr. Bullinger in his book "Number in Scripture," page 285, states that the gematria of this one verse ("gematria" means tallying up all the numerical value of the letter in the verse) comes to 4,662, which

45

answers to 7 times 666!" (Martin, *101 Bible Secrets that Christians Do Not Know*, pg. 52)

These numerical relationships are not there by chance. They have meaning to them and it is up to us to find out what those meanings are.

Interesting Relationships Between Books
or Parts of Books in Scripture

I could point out many interesting relationships between and among books or parts of books, but I am only in this regard going to mention one very interesting one. This fact is almost wholly unknown and the only commentator that I have ever seen discuss it is my late father. It concerns the connection and the obvious relationship between Psalms 103-106. It is not obvious to us if we have not studied these Psalms carefully, but there is a clue beyond just the fact that when you read these four Psalms in order, you find they are obviously connected. But where is the clue that brings this fact out into the open?

Note my late father's discussion of this issue saying:

"The four Psalms which record King David's "History of the World" are 103, 104, 105 and 106. There is a common theme (chronologically arranged) which systematically goes from one important event to another linking them together in an historical context until the time when King David deposited the Ark of the Covenant in its sacred repository on Mount Zion. All four of these Psalms must have been written to celebrate that significant event because they agree substantially with a Psalm composed at that time (I Chronicles 16:7-36). Note that the first 15 verses of Psalm 105 tally almost exactly with David's composite Psalm recorded in First Chronicles 16:7-36 in honor of the Ark of the Covenant, while the last two verses of Psalm 106 also agree with the last verses of the Psalm in Chronicles." (Martin, The Post Flood Creations of God, Portland: OR, ASK Publications, pg. 11)

These four Psalms are absolutely connected together, but we don't think through the possibility that they could be connected. My late father studied these things very carefully and came up with some thought provoking ideas. What this shows is that we need to pay careful attention to Scripture because we may find more than meets the eye and that we need to dig deeper and pay closer attention to the Bible in detail.

How does this relate to the book of Hebrews?

Hebrews is a very different type of book and it was written to certain people at a certain time for a certain reason, but Paul is not open about who he is addressing or where they were located. He does not openly mention Jerusalem or the land of Israel. He may have had a serious reason for doing that. He may be using similar techniques like Jeremiah talking about "Sheshak" instead of Babylon.

What we are going to find later in this book is that Paul did use some terms to identify the recipients of the book which would have only been understood by people who were spiritually in tune with the Hebrew Bible and who were also very in tune with the geography of Jerusalem and in particular that associated with the Holy Temple. The way that this material is introduced and the language it is couched in is very spiritual language, but make no mistake about it, these terms and phrases that Paul used to help identify the recipients of this letter are clear and easy to

47

understand to those who were in tune with and familiar with Jerusalem's geography and that of the design, layout and compartments of the Holy Temple as well. We will see this demonstrated shortly.

What we must understand about the book of Hebrews is that it is one of Paul's more complex writings. It is really "post graduate work" when it comes to studying the New Testament. It is not to just be referred to haphazardly out of context. One needs very serious study to learn the truth of this most difficult letter. This is even attested by St. Peter who in speaking about St. Paul's writings said the following:

"Therefore, beloved, since you are waiting for these, be diligent to be found by him without spot or blemish, and at peace. And count the patience of our Lord as salvation, just as our beloved brother Paul also wrote to you according to the wisdom given him, as he does in all his letters when he speaks in them of these matters. There are some things in them that are hard to understand, which the ignorant and unstable twist to their own destruction, as they do the other Scriptures. You therefore, beloved, knowing this beforehand, take care that you are not carried away with the error of lawless people and lose your own stability." (II Peter 3:14-17 ESV)

This is a super important text. We know that Peter's ministry was to the Circumcision, to Jewish believers. (Galatians 2:8). He also wrote his two letters to "elect exiles of the Dispersion" (Greek: *Diaspora*) (I Peter 1:1; II Peter 3:1). These references show that Peter was writing to Jewish/Hebrew believers and this is exactly to whom he notes Paul also wrote "to you". This shows clearly that Paul wrote a letter to the Jewish/Hebrew believers and there seems to be little doubt that we have that letter in our New Testament.

48

Before further discussion on this point, let us first review the dating for Hebrews and when it was originally composed.

4

When was the book of Hebrews written?

In this book, this question has a simple answer. We can start with an overall question saying: Was the book of Hebrews written before AD 70 when the Temple in Jerusalem was destroyed (a well-known historical benchmark)? In this regard, the best evidence of a long standing historical opinion favors the view that all of the books of the New Testament could have been written before AD 70.

This view is well attested in the book by Prof. J.A.T Robinson titled: *"Redating the New Testament."* My late father refers to this in his book *"Restoring the Original Bible"*:

"There is also the question of the exact times John wrote his Gospel and three epistles. The Gospel seems to be a late production, though John's mention of five porches as seemingly in existence in Jerusalem (5:3) and the reference that Peter "will" be martyred (21:19) might indicate the basic writing of the Gospel was early, even before the destruction of Jerusalem. Prof. J.A.T. Robinson, in his excellent book *Redating the New Testament*, thought this to be the case."[16]

---

[16] Martin, Ernest L., *Restoring the Original Bible*, Portland, OR: ASK Publications. 1994. P.411

John's books were not the only books that Professor Robinson believed were written before AD 70. In fact, Professor Robinson believed that all of the books of the New Testament were indeed written before AD 70, which is the view we accept herein.

But what about the book of Hebrews? When was it written? An important view in this regard is expressed in CBTEL. Note it here:

"Assuming the Pauline authorship of the epistle, it is not difficult to determine when and where it was written. The allusions in xiii, 19,21, point to the closing period of the apostle's two years' imprisonment at Rome as the season during 'the serene hours' of which, as Hug describes them (*Introd.* p. 603), he composed this noblest production of his pen. Modern criticism has not destroyed, though it has weakened this conclusion, by substituting the reading τοῖς δεσμίοις, 'the prisoners,' for τοῖς δεσμίοις μου (A.V. 'me in my bonds'), x.34; by proposing to interpret ἀπολελυμένον, xiii, 23, as 'sent away' rather than 'set at liberty:' and by urging that the condition of the writer, as portrayer in xiii. 18, 19, 23, is not necessarily that of a prisoner, and that there may possibly be no allusion to it in xiii.3. In this date, however, almost all who receive the epistle as Paul's concur; and even by those who do not so receive it nearly the same time is fixed upon, in consequence of the evidence furnished by the epistle itself of its having been written a good while after those to whom it is addressed had become Christians. The references to former teachers (xiii.7) and earlier instructions (v.12 and x.32) might suit any time after the first years of the Church; **but the epistle was evidently written before the destruction of Jerusalem in A.D. 70**. The whole argument, and especially the passages viii.4 sq., ix.6 sq. (where the present tenses of the Greek are unaccountably changed into

51

past in the English version), and xiii.10 sq. **imply that the Temple was standing**, and that its usual course of divine service was carried on without interruption."[17]

CBTEL's commentators are relying on abundant ancient evidence as Lardner relays in *Credibility* making note of the early opinions of Clement of Alexandria, Jerome, Euthalius, Chrysostom, Theodoret, and Theophylact[18] who agree that:

"Those exhortations, ch. xiii.13,14, must have been very suitable to the case of the Jews of Jerusalem, at the supposed time of writing this epistle, **a few years before the war in that country (e.g. in A.D. 70) that broke out** ."[19]

Later scholars quoted by Lardner also affirm similar dating. Note the uniform dating:

"Thus we are brought to the fourth and last part of our inquiry concerning this epistle, the time and place of writing it. Mill was of opinion, that this epistle was written by Paul in the year 63, in some part of Italy, soon after he had been released from his imprisonment at Rome. Mr. Wetstein appears to have been of the same opinion. Tillemont likewise placeth this epistle in the year 63, immediately after the apostle's being set at liberty;

---

[17] M'Clintock, Rev. John , D.D., & Strong, James, S.T.D. Cyclopedia of Biblical, Theological and Ecclesiastical Literature, New York: Harper & Brothers Publishers, 1883. Vol. IV, pg. 147.

[18] Lardner, Nathaniel, "The Credibility of the Gospel History; or the Principal Facts of the New Testament confirmed by Passages of Ancient Authors, who were contemporary with our Saviour or his Apostles, or lived near their time.", London: William Ball, 1838. Vol. VI, pg. 81

[19] *ibid.*, pg. 82.

who, as he says, was still in Rome, or at least in Italy. Banage speak of this epistle at the year 61, and supposeth it to be written during the apostle's imprisonment. For he afterward speaks of the epistle to the Ephesians, and says, it was the last letter, which the apostle wrote during the time of his bounds. L'Enfant & Beausobre, in their general preface to St. Paul's epistles, observe that in the subscription at the end of the epistle it is said to have been written from Italy. The only ground of which, as they add, is what is said, ch. 13.24. 'They of Italy salute you.'[20]

To conclude, I can comment on the view my late father held on when Hebrews was written. He believed that Hebrews was written in the early part of A.D. 61.[21]

What we will focus on in this book is the idea that Hebrews was composed and transmitted to the recipients before 70AD and the case for that date is a strong one.

---

[20] *ibid.* pgs. 109-110
[21] Martin, Ernest L., *Restoring the Original Bible*, Portland, OR: ASK Publications. 1994. P.185

5

To whom and to what geographical region was the book of Hebrews written?

One of the most interesting factors about looking at commentators on Hebrews especially among Christians today who use Hebrews to prove to Christians the necessity today to spank children, they generally just home in on Hebrews 12:5-11 and give no other consideration for the context of Hebrews 12, its relation to the rest of the book and the book as a whole not to mention how the book relates to the other books in St. Paul's collection. They never seem to question who the book was written to also in the first place. They just identify "Christians" as the subject people with little elaboration or definition.

Unfortunately, this is a very superficial and frankly a very poor approach to seeking a wide and comprehensive view on this book with the goal to better understanding its messages. One of my friends, Pastor Crystal Lutton, characterizes Hebrews as the most abused book in all of the New Testament because its teachings are often misapplied. I agree with this very much and it is in this line that we have to ask ourselves who were the people to whom this book was written to in the first place?

Understanding to whom the book of Hebrews was written is a fundamentally important question. To begin, let us understand that the title of the book, *"To Hebrews"* (πρὸς Ἑβραίους) is very ancient. Note the reference in this regard from Thomas Newberry from the Newberry Study Bible (p.330 in the New Testament segment) saying:

"Inscription – ℵABDE state to whom it was written, ..."

This very short assertion shows that the five out of the six oldest manuscripts, which are designated in the field of New Testament Textual Criticism with these five letters (ℵABDE), of the New Testament (Siniaticus (ℵ), Alexandrinus (A), Vaticanus (B), Bezae (D) and Basileennsis (E) all have this above referenced title (*"To Hebrews"* πρὸς Ἑβραίους).

CBTEL also comments on this issue saying:

"The inscription of the epistle, πρὸς Ἑβραίους, (*To Hebrews*) which is of great antiquity, ..." (vol. VI, pg. 147)

CBTEL continues to show that it was addressed specifically to Jewish Christians, focusing on the community at or near Jerusalem:

"That the parties to whom this epistle was addressed were converted Jews the epistle itself plainly shows. Ancient tradition points out the church at Jerusalem, or the Christians in Palestine generally, as the recipients. ... Two things make this clear, says Lange: the one is, that only the Christians in Jerusalem, or those in Palestine generally, formed a great Jewish-Christian Church in the proper sense; the other is, that for the loosening of those from their religious sense of the Temple-worship, there was an immediate and pressing necessity. (*Apostol Zeitalter*, I, 176). We know of no purely Jewish Christian community, such as that addressed in this epistle, out of

Palestine, while the whole tone of the epistle that those for whom it was intended were in the vicinity of the Temple." (*ibid.*)

In discussing specifically the inscription of the epistle, πρός Ἑβραίους, (*To Hebrews*) with Professor Stephen Pfann, he suggested that due to the subject matter of the book and to those to whom it was addressed, a more accurate title could be *"To Hebrew Christians."* I think his suggestion makes excellent sense. Clearly, we are not speaking about just any group of people having a Hebrew heritage. Not at all. The recipients of this letter are Hebrew Christians without question.

This is a very important quote which we will elaborate on further shortly. However, further testimonies as to the target group for the book of Hebrews are necessary here:

"Chrysostom says that the epistle was sent to the believing Jews of Palestine. And supposeth, that the apostle afterwards made them a visit. Theodoret in his preface to the epistle allows it to be sent to the same Jews. And Theophylact in his argument of the epistle expressly says, as Chrysostom, that it was sent to the Jews of Palestine. So that this was the general opinion of the ancients." (Lardner, *Credibility*, vol. VI, pg. 81.)

Continuing with the following very relevant information in this regard:

"2. There are in the epistle many things especially suitable to the believers in Judea. Which must lead us to think it was written to them. I shall select divers such passages.

1.) Hebr. 1.2, - "Has in these last days spoken unto us by his Son."

2.) Ch. iv. 2, "For unto us was the gospel preached, as well as to them."

3.) Ch. ii. 1-4, "Therefore we ought to give the more earnest heed to the things that we have heard ------- how then shall we escape, if we neglect to great salvation, which at the first began to be spoken by the Lord, and was confirmed unto us by them that heard him; God also bearing them witness with signs and wonders, and with divers miracles, and gifts of the Holy Ghost."

Does not that exhortation, and the reason, with which it is supported, peculiarly suit the believers in Judea, where Christ himself first taught, and then his disciples after him, confirming their testimony with very numerous and conspicuous miracles?

4.) The people, to whom this epistle is sent, were well acquainted with our Saviour's sufferings, as they of Judea must have been. This appears in ch. I, 3; ii.9, 18; v.7, 8; ix.14; x.11; xii. 2, 3; xiii. 12.

5.) Ch. v.12. "For when ye ought to be teachers of others," and what follows is most properly understood of Christians in Jerusalem and Judea, to whom the gospel was first preached.

6.) What is said, ch. iv. 4-6, and x. 20-29, is most properly applicable to apostates in Judea.

7.) Ch. x. 32-34, "But call to remembrance the former days, in which, after ye were illuminated, ye endured a great flight of afflictions ------- to the end of ver. 34. This leads us to the church of Jerusalem, which had suffered much, long before the writing this epistle, even very soon after they had received the knowledge of the truth. Comp. Acts viii. 1; ix. 1, 2; xi. 19; and I Thess, ii.14. Grotius supposeth as much.

8.) Those exhortations, ch. xiii. 13, 14, must have been very suitable to the case of the Jews of Jerusalem, at the supposed time of writing this epistle, as few years before the war in that country broke out.

9.) The regard show in this epistle to the rulers of the church or churches, to which it is sent, is very remarkable. They are mentioned twice or thrice; first in ch. xiii. 7, "Remember your rulers, who have spoken unto you the word of God: whose faith imitate, considering the end of their conversation." These were dead, as Grotius observes. And Theodoret's note is to this purpose: He intends the saints that were dead, Stephen the proto-martyr, James the brother of John, and James called the Just. And there were many others, ... Consider these, says he, and observing their example, imitate their faith.' Then again in ver. 17, Obey them that have the rule of over, and submit yourselves. For they watch for your souls." ----------- And once more, ver. 24, "Salute all them that have the rule over you, and all the saints." Upon which Theodoret says: 'This way of speaking intimates, that their rulers did not need such instruction. For which reason he did not write to them, but to their disciples.' This is a fine observation. And Whitby upon that verse, says: 'Hence, it seems evident, that this epistle was not sent to the bishops or rulers of the church, but to the whole church or the laity.' And it may deserve to be considered, whether this repeated notice of the rulers among them does not afford ground to believe, that some of the apostles were in Judea? Whether there be sufficient reason to believe that, or not, I think these notices very and suitable to the state of the Jewish believers in Judea. For I am persuaded, that not only, James, and all the other apostles, had exactly the same doctrine with Paul; but that all the elders likewise, and all the understanding men among the Jewish believers, embraced the same doctrine. They were, as I apprehend, the multitude only, πλῆθος plebs, or the men of lower rank among them, who were attached to the peculiarities of the Mosaic law, and the customs of their ancestors. This may be argued from what James and the elders at Jerusalem say to Paul. Acts xxi.20-22. "Thou seest, brother, how many thousands of Jews there are that believe. And they are all zealous of the law. ----------What is it therefore? The multitude must needs come together." ------ It is hence evident, that the zeal for the law, which prevailed in the minds of many, was not approved by James, or the elders. That being the case, these recommendations of a regard for their rulers, whether apostles, or elders, were very proper in an epistle sent to the believers in Judea.

For these reasons I think that this epistle was sent to the Jewish believers at Jerusalem, and in Judea." (*ibid.* pg. 81-83)

This is a powerful quote from Lardner which weaves in very reasonable Scriptural exposition with numerous ancient testimonies and contemporary scholarship in his time (late 18th century).

Lardner also notes the view of the eminent Bible scholar Lightfoot:

"Lightfoot thought, 'That this epistle was sent by Paul to the believing Jews of Judea, a people, says he, that had been much engaged to him, for his are of their poor, getting collections for them all along in his travels.' He adds: 'It is not to be doubted, in deed, that he intended the discourse and matter of this epistle to the Jews throughout their dispersion – Yet he does endorse it, and send it chiefly to the Hebrew, or the Jews of Judea, the

59

principal part of the circumcision, as the properest centre to which to direct it, and from whence it might be best dispersed in time to the whole circumference of the dispersion." (pg.80)

Continuing:

"Whitby, in his preface to the epistle to the Hebrews, is of the same opinion, and argues after the same manner with Lightfoot." (*ibid.*)

Lardner really was one of the greatest expositors of the New Testament in the last 300 years. He really helps us get back into the original material of the Greek and Latin Fathers of the Early Church.

To this quote, we need also to add the following information, which is essential to cement the idea that this letter of Hebrews was indeed sent to Jewish believers in Jesus in Jerusalem or to Jewish believers who had an intimate knowledge of the geography of Jerusalem especially around the immediate region of the Holy Temple.

"Outside the Camp"

Earlier we had mentioned the following saying ("outside the camp"). We mentioned that Paul did use some terms to identify the recipients of the book of Hebrews, which would have only been understood by people who were spiritually in tune with the Hebrew Bible and who were also very knowledgeable of the geography of Jerusalem and in particular that associated with the Holy Temple. The overall scholarly consensus favors Jerusalem and the believers who lived there as the recipients of the book of Hebrews. There is, though, in addition to the evidence we are presenting here, a very convincing proof which demonstrates this even further adding in some more specific geographical keys. These keys today can be read right over by someone not aware of or familiar with the geography that existed in Jerusalem in the time of Christ. The nature of this evidence is very important and it is easily missed. Let's consider this.

In this regard, we need to review Hebrews 13: 10-14:

"We have an altar from which those who serve the tabernacle have no right to eat. For the bodies of those animals whose blood is brought into the holy place by the high priest as an offering for sin, are burned outside the camp. Therefore Jesus also, that He might sanctify the people through His own blood, suffered outside the gate. So, let us go out to Him outside the camp, bearing His reproach. For here we do not have a lasting city, but we are seeking the city which is to come." (NASB)

Commenting on this text, my late father, Dr. Ernest L. Martin, who was one of the world's top experts on the geography of Jerusalem in the time of Christ (studying under the eminent Israeli archaeologist, the late Professor Benjamin Mazar among many others), said the following with particular reference to an article produced by the late Professor Helmut Koester of Harvard Divinity School:

"The first thing that must be recognized is that a literal altar is being discussed by the author of Hebrews. It has been abundantly proved by Helmut Koester ("Outside the Camp," Harvard Theological Review. 1962 (55), pp.299-315) that the "altar" cannot be a symbol for the Lord's Supper nor is it a figure of speech for the "cross" of Christ. After all, the "bodies of those beasts" were literal, the "blood brought into the sanctuary" was literal, the "high priest" was literal, the sin offerings that were "burned outside the

61

camp" were literal, and the fact that the priests "had no right to eat" of those particular sin offerings was also literal, so why shouldn't "the altar" itself be literal? The truth is, the altar being discussed in the Book of Hebrews was a well-known holy place to the inhabitants of Jerusalem in the time of Christ. It was a specific altar located outside the camp of Jerusalem where certain sin offerings were burnt to ashes. It will pay us to rehearse what these sin offerings were because the Book of Hebrews singles them out as symbolically referring to Christ when he became the great sin offering for the whole world at the time of his crucifixion."[22]

What this text in Hebrews 13:10-14 along with this explanation shows is that we have some geographical descriptions here which are unmistakably found in a Jerusalem context. In fact, they are meaningless outside of a Jerusalem geographical context found in a Temple oriented environment with the Hebrew Scriptures as our guide. To a first century Jewish believer living in Jerusalem in the time of our Lord Jesus, this text is full of meaning. But it is also easy to see how without an intimate knowledge of the particulars of the geography around the Temple in the time of Jesus, this text appears to be a very nice spiritualization of the crucifixion of Jesus. Nothing could be farther from the truth.

Additional information about this important site in Jerusalem is further discussed by my late father saying:

"Note that Ezekiel located this altar outside the actual Temple. It was positioned inside "the house" (Hebrew: ha-Beth and in the Talmud it was called Beth ha-Deshen, the House of the Ashes). The name Miphkad associated with this altar tells us that it was a place of "the Muster"

---

[22] Martin, Secrets of Golgotha, ASK Publications: Portland: OR, 1994, pg. 28

(Numbering or Census). The word Miphkad is sometimes mistakenly rendered "appointed place," but it is the untranslated word that should be retained in Ezekiel. The actual meaning of the word is "Numbering Place" or "the Place of the Muster."

The location of the Miphkad (and the altar for burning the sin offerings which was in "the house") is most important regarding the matter of the crucifixion because the Book of Hebrews identifies it as the area of the altar associated with Christ's death. Strangely, the majority of biblical scholars seldom mention that such an altar existed in the time of Christ or that it had a major part to play in the Temple worship at Jerusalem. But the altar at the Miphkad was as holy and significant as was the Altar of Burnt Offering in the outer court of the Temple and the Golden Incense Altar within the Holy Place. The author of the Book of Hebrews, however, said that this altar had real Christian symbolism attached to it and that it was the one located "outside the gate" and "outside the camp." He advised all Christians allegorically to go out to Christ at that altar. What is important to realize is that the Book of Hebrews is referring to a literal altar which was well known to the people of Jerusalem in the time of Christ. And where was it located? Without doubt, that altar for burning the sin offerings to ashes was situated on the Mount of Olives. It was the altar at the Miphkad mentioned in Ezekiel 43:21." (*ibid.* pg. 38-39)

What this significant evidence points to very convincingly is that this information in Hebrews points to the site of our Lord Jesus' crucifixion, which was called an "altar" in Hebrews 13:10 and that the evidence points very strongly to the facts that Hebrews was indeed written to those living in and intimately familiar with the area of Jerusalem around the area of the Holy Temple.

63

There is another topic found in Hebrews which has a direct geographical link to the land of Israel and the people living in that land. This subject also has a close link to the issue of corporal punishment/spanking/smacking. This subject is the issue of tithing, or giving ten percent of one's income to God's work. It may seem strange to link these two subjects, but when we study this subject of tithing further, we will find that many of the mistakes made in properly understanding the issue of corporal punishment/spanking/smacking are the same mistakes made surrounding the issue of tithing. We will review this issue shortly.

Tithing and its relevance to the land of Israel and Torah Observant Jews

Tithing is one other teaching in the book of Hebrews which very much helps link the book of Hebrews to a Jewish, Hebraic context situated in the land of Israel. It may seem strange to those who have not carefully studied the matter of tithing (which includes most of those who even adhere to the practice in my experience), but when one does, this fact becomes highly relevant and it affects what we know and understand about the letter to the Hebrews even in a geographical sense. Of course, most Christians today make no distinctions about tithing because it is almost universally taught in Christendom today that tithing as a teaching which is binding on Christians today, but there is almost no real expository Bible teaching surrounding this issue. Unfortunately advocates of tithing today for Christians are 100% mistaken and are misapplying a teaching that was given in a Law of Moses, Hebraic context and was only really applicable initially to the Land of Israel and concerned only the increase of agricultural products and animals in the land. Tithing on 10% of your income across the board for all Christians is a false teaching that needs to be jettisoned. Unfortunately, this teaching is entrenched in Christian teaching today and the poorest among us, who are not excused from tithing, are those hurt the most by this teaching which is one of the most misunderstood and destructive in all Christendom.

Tithing (like corporal punishment/spanking/smacking) is another one of those "clear and plain Biblical teachings" that Christians just take for granted never to be studied in depth. Concerning tithing, I am very grateful to my late father, Dr. Ernest L. Martin, for his groundbreaking work on the tithing issue.

This is an important matter because many churches and denominations that promote spanking/smacking/corporal punishment also believe in tithing and both of these subjects are linked to the book of Hebrews. I know this well because the church that I grew up in practiced extreme forms of both of these teachings. I think that many Christians will also share this experience.

What we will find is that the teaching of tithing helps us establish to whom this book was sent in the first place and how it was relevant for them, but also how it, like spanking/smacking children, is no longer relevant for us Christians today.

For more information on the subject of tithing and its links to corporal punishment/spanking/smacking, please see Appendix One in this book.

6

Is Hebrews targeting those falling away from the Christian faith?

In the earlier part of this book, I quoted a passage from a Christian advocate of corporal punishment who frames his discussion about spanking children by saying the following about the book of Hebrews:

"Let's begin by looking at one of the foundational passages related to parental discipline in the NT: Hebrews 12:4–11. The context is that the author is addressing Christians who are suffering." (see footnote 3)

This is the main introduction that this brother in Christ gives in seeking to frame his discussion and advocacy surrounding the issue of spanking/smacking children.

He identifies this text as "one of the foundational passages related to parental discipline in the NT (New Testament). He also says that "the context is that the author is addressing Christians who are suffering."

What we will find, though, in this previously mentioned paper is a heavy emphasis on why Christians today should spank/smack their children on the basis of this text, but zero analysis of the true context of the passages, the fact that this book is written to Hebrew oriented, Torah observant Hebrew Christians living in Jerusalem, plus no analysis of the context in which the book was written or its main message.

What this author is showing is that this text in Hebrews 12:5-11 is a "foundational passage" surrounding the need to spank/smack your children. What we have to ask ourselves though is: How firm is the foundation on which this dear brother in Christ is building his theological teachings on?

Now, let us be clear about what the book of Hebrews overall teaches. In this case, my dear brother in Christ is partially correct. The "Christians" are "suffering" in Hebrews. Let's see this demonstrated clearly from the text itself.

First, let us understand (as we are asserting in this book) that the recipients of the letter to the Hebrews were Hebrew Christians living in Jerusalem who were just on the verge of giving up their faith. Notice Hebrews 12:4, which says:

"In your struggle against sin you have not yet resisted to the point of shedding your blood." (ESV)

These Hebrew Christians had been believers for a long time, but they were retreating back into immaturity in the faith. Note Hebrews 5:11-14:

"About this we have much to say, and it is hard to explain, since you have become dull of hearing. For though by this time you ought to be teachers, you need someone to teach you again the basic principles of the oracles of God. You need milk, not solid food, for everyone who lives on milk is unskilled in the word of righteousness, since he is a child. But solid food is for the mature, for those who have their powers of discernment trained by constant practice to distinguish good from evil." (ESV)

What was happening to these Hebrew Christians is that many of them were thinking of giving up their faith. Note these texts which show this quite convincingly.

"but Christ is faithful over God's house as a son. And we are his house, **if indeed we hold fast our confidence and our boasting in our hope.**" (Hebrews 3:6 ESV)

"Take care, brothers, lest **there be in any of you an evil, unbelieving heart, leading you to fall away from the living God.**" (Hebrews 3:12 ESV)

"But exhort one another every day, as long as it is called "today," **that none of you may be hardened by the deceitfulness of sin.**" (Hebrews 3:12 ESV)

"As it is said, "Today, if you hear his voice, **do not harden your hearts as in the rebellion.**" (Hebrews 3:15 ESV)

"Therefore, while the promise of entering his rest still stands, let us fear **lest any of you should seem to have failed to reach it.**" (Hebrews 4:1 ESV)

"again he appoints a certain day, "Today," saying through David so long afterward, in the words already quoted, "Today, if you hear his voice, **do not harden your hearts.**" (Hebrews 4:7 ESV) "for whoever has entered God's rest has also rested from his works as God did from his. Let us therefore strive to enter that rest, **so that no one may fall by the same sort of disobedience.**" (Hebrews 4:10-11 ESV)

There is no mistaking the problems that were present among this community of Hebrew Christians. People among them had fallen back doctrinally.

"And **we desire each one of you to show the same earnestness to have the full assurance of hope until the end, so that you may not be sluggish, but imitators of those who through faith and patience inherit the promises.** For when God made a promise to Abraham, since he had no one greater by whom to swear, he swore by himself, saying, "Surely I will bless you and multiply you." And thus Abraham, **having patiently waited, obtained the promise.** (Hebrews 6:11-15 ESV)

Paul again in Chapter ten again urges them to **"hold fast to their confession:"**

"Let us hold fast the confession of our hope without wavering, for he who promised is faithful." (10:23 ESV)

Paul once again urges them not to throw away their confidence (e.g. their faith) saying:

"But **recall the former days** when, **after you were enlightened,** you endured a hard struggle with sufferings, sometimes being publicly exposed to reproach and affliction, and sometimes being partners with those so treated. For you had compassion on those in prison, and you joyfully accepted the plundering of your property, since you knew that you yourselves had a better possession and an abiding one. Therefore **do not throw away your confidence**, which has a great reward. For **you have need of endurance**, so that when you have done the will of God you may receive what is promised. For yet a little while, and the coming one will come and will not delay; but **my righteous one shall live by faith**, and **if he shrinks back, my soul has no pleasure in him.**"

But **we are not of those who shrink back and are destroyed**, but **of those who have faith and preserve their souls.**" (10:32-39 ESV)

After this, what do we find taking place? The most extensive chapter in the entire Bible dedicated to the matter of faith. Of course, there would be no need to rehearse this teaching to a community under no pressure or facing no test of their faith. Hardly! The Apostle is introducing this chapter to strengthen their faith because it was in a much weakened condition due to the circumstances that they were facing. Look at what the Apostle tells them about finally how so many other suffered:

"And what more shall I say? For time would fail me to tell of Gideon, Barak, Samson, Jephthah, of David and Samuel and the prophets— who through faith conquered kingdoms, enforced justice, obtained promises, stopped the mouths of lions, quenched the power of fire, escaped the edge of the sword, **were made strong out of weakness**, became mighty in war, put foreign armies to flight. Women received back their dead by resurrection. Some were tortured, refusing to accept release, **so that they**

might rise again to a better life. Others suffered mocking and flogging, and even chains and imprisonment. They were stoned, they were sawn in two they were killed with the sword. They went about in skins of sheep and goats, destitute, afflicted, mistreated— of whom the world was not worthy—wandering about in deserts and mountains, and in dens and caves of the earth." Hebrews 11:32-38 ESV)

This section at the end of Hebrews 11 is linked to the start of Hebrews 12 which says:

"Therefore, since we are surrounded by so great a cloud of witnesses, **let us also lay aside every weight**, and sin which clings so closely, and **let us run with endurance the race that is set before us**, looking to Jesus, the founder and perfecter of our faith, **who for the joy that was set before him endured the cross**, despising the shame, and is seated at the right hand of the throne of God." (Hebrews 12:1-2 ESV)

So, here at the end, the Apostle is telling his readers to repent, to look towards Christ and to endure.

Finally, in the first part of Hebrews 12, we have this final exhortation to endure and be patient saying:

"Consider him **who endured** from sinners such hostility against himself, so that **you may not grow weary or fainthearted**." (Hebrews 12:3 ESV)

What we can see in the book of Hebrews is indeed a letter directed to Christians who are "suffering." While this is true, it is not really appropriate to compare this suffering of those Hebrew Christians in

71

Jerusalem to all Christians in general. The circumstances that those people found themselves in, the beliefs that they had and the situations that they faced do not equally compare to Christians today living outside of Israel and not following the same "zeal" for the Mosaic Law that those believers had.

7

What is the main subject of the book of Hebrews?

I think that we can all agree based on objective evidence that the book of Hebrews is a little different than St. Paul's other books. I think we also can agree that the book of Hebrews contains the truth. The book of Hebrews is, however, as we have seen herein, different than the other letters in St. Paul's collection. What we need to ascertain is: Whose truth is it? How relevant does it remain today in the life of Christians, particularly of Gentile Christians? On the surface, these may seem like strange questions, but in this research study, we are taking this matter to be one of supreme relevance. To some Christian authorities today, it is their right to just quote Hebrews in any way they wish with no consideration for its original context and meaning. How mistaken and unfortunate this is.

To begin to understand Hebrews and its teachings better, one of the key things we really need to understand is what the main subject of the book of Hebrews itself is. What is this book trying to teach? Why was it written? What was it communicating? This is not an easy subject to understand because St. Paul chose to introduce the subject of this book in a way which is not expected and this is why I have mentioned some interesting literary devices or other ways to transmit information that we have in the Bible. What we are going to find is something similar in how the subject of the book of Hebrews is introduced. It is done so in a very subtle way. This is in direct opposition to many Christian pastors who will have us believe that the reason for Hebrews to be written is to provide them evidence to support spanking/smacking children. This, unfortunately, is how this most important book of Hebrews today is treated by many mistaken Christian leaders, pastors and Bible teachers.

I have read quite a few articles about Hebrews and its supposed advocacy for corporal punishment, but very few people ever think it necessary to explain what the book is about in the first place. It is almost as if today Christian advocates of spanking pull out their "go to" texts in Hebrews in the New Testament to "prove" spanking.

Let us look now at how St. Paul does this. Let us look at the key text which introduces the overall subject of Hebrews. It is found in Hebrews 2:5 saying:

"For it was not to angels that God subjected *__the world to come__*, **of which we are speaking.**" (ESV)

This translation gives an excellent view into the subject of the whole book of Hebrews overall. You can almost miss it if you are not in tune with the main subject of the book and the context into which it is written. It may seem strange to say, but "the World to Come" or the Millennial reign of Christ on this earth is the main subject of this book, but this is what we are suggesting in this book following the suggestion of my late father, Dr. Ernest L. Martin, who proposed this idea.

When we use this little key to unlock the door of the teachings of Hebrews (coupled with a number of other teachings we have referenced herein), a message about this book starts to present itself which concerns

74

the issue of the Millennium and the fact that St. Paul was giving forth a message to a certain group of Hebrew Christians concerning this issue of 'the world to come' or the Millennial Age of 1,000 year's time to begin immediately following the return of Jesus Christ back to this earth. When we realize this, we start to see some very specific teachings fall into place which help us hopefully to better understand this book and its information.

The Position of Hebrews in the
Original Manuscripts of the New Testament

As we have mentioned earlier, in the earliest and best manuscript evidence we have, the book of Hebrews appears in the New Testament following II Thessalonians and before First Timothy. This is significant. This is because when we review the subject matter of the letters to the Thessalonians, we find there is a great deal of emphasis and information in those letters about the time just before our Lord Jesus returns to this earth. Anyone who reads both of those letters to the Thessalonians will notice very clearly the subjects dealing with the coming of Christ.

Note that some people associated with the Thessalonian Church were believing that the day of the Lord had already come. (II Thessalonians 2:2) Paul said that was not so. What though would be the next logical subject to discuss after discussing subjects dealing with the time just before Jesus Christ returns to earth from heaven? Of course, it would be the time period just after Jesus returns and that is what we have following the letters to the Thessalonians as referenced in the book of Hebrews.

The World to Come (Christ's 1,000 Year Reign):
The Main Subject of Hebrews

Now, when you normally open a book, you introduce the main subject, but in Hebrews it is a little bit different and the subject of the book is introduced following an introductory section. However, if we pay close attention to the information we find even in the first few verses of Hebrews, we may find further validation that the subject of the book is "The World to Come." Let's look at the first few verses of Hebrews and see what it may be telling us:

"Long ago, at many times and in many ways, God spoke to our fathers by the prophets, but in these last days he has spoken to us by his Son, whom he appointed the heir of all things, through whom also he created the world." (Hebrews 1:1-2 ESV)

These verses don't seem to be too millennially oriented, but wait a moment. Maybe they are more millennial than we might think. We will consider this issue in detail shortly.

The first thing though that we must understand about the context of the time period when Hebrews was written is that the people to whom it was written, Jewish believers in Jesus as the Messiah, generally believed that Jesus would be returning from heaven in their lifetimes. This is important to understand. Let's review some of the evidence. Here I want to refer to an article written by my late father, Dr. Ernest L. Martin, titled: "*The Expectation of Christ's Second Coming in Apostolic Times.*" In this article, my father noted the following in the five below referenced quotes:

1. "There was a profound belief in the minds of the apostles that Christ would establish His Messianic kingdom during their lifetimes. "There be some standing here, which shall not taste of

76

death, till they see the Son of Man coming in his kingdom." (Matt. 16:28).

2. "And though Christ, after His resurrection, emphasized that "it is not for you to know the times or the seasons, which the Father has put in his own power" (Acts 1:7), the apostles continued to mention Christ's second coming as imminent until the year A.D. 63."

3. The 70 Weeks Prophecy of Daniel 9:24-27 provided much of the evidence that the Apostles initially relied on concerning Christ's Second Advent – "Since Daniel wrote the prophecy in the latter part of the 500's B.C., there was a general understanding that the Messiah would establish His kingdom on earth near the first century B.C. or the first century A.D.. The historical records reflect this belief. Josephus mentioned that it was found in the "sacred writings that about that time one from their country [Judaea] should become governor of the habitable earth" (Josephus, Wars, VI, 313). The Roman historians of the first century were also aware of the prophecy: "A firm belief had long prevailed through the East that it was destined for the empire of the world at that time to be given to someone who should go forth from Judaea"(Suetonius, Vespasian, iv).

4. Tacitus also said: "The majority of the Jewish people were very impressed with the belief that it was contained in ancient writings of the priests that it would come to pass that at that very time, the East would renew its strength and they that should go forth from Judaea should be rulers of the world" (Tacitus, History, v. 13). Even the Roman Emperor Nero was advised by one or two of his court astrologers that it was prudent for him to move his seat of

empire to Jerusalem because that city was then destined to become the capital city of the world (Suetonius, Nero, 40)."

5. "The apostles were assured (and correctly) that the Immanuel of the virgin birth was Jesus. He had grown into manhood and was crucified (according to prophecy) in A.D. 30. Three days later He was resurrected from the dead. He was now a glorified being and ready to take over His role as the King of Israel. The time for the arrival of the Messianic kingdom of Daniel and Isaiah looked very near. Since the apostles were aware that Christ was born in the fall of 3 B.C. (and that He was certainly the Immanuel born of the virgin), 65 years from that nativity directed them to A.D. 63. Since Isaiah had already said that the length of a king's reign was 70 years (Isa. 23:15) - and the Messiah was to be a king - the apostles must have thought that within 70 years of Christ's birth (65 years to be exact) the Messianic kingdom would have to arise." (edits mine)

However, just around the time when Hebrews was written in its first initial draft, this was a time when Paul and Peter began to understand that the Second Coming of Christ would not take place in their lifetimes. The evidence for this is found here in the present book of our discussion and in II Peter, which is closely linked to the book of Hebrews.

The Link between the books of II Peter and the book of Hebrews
As we have said earlier, the overall subject matter of the book of Hebrews concerns the World to Come or the Millennial reign of our Lord Jesus Christ. Now, it is no coincidence that Peter also spoke about this issue addressing the same general group of people that Paul was addressing in Hebrews: Jewish Christians! Yes, Peter tells us in II Peter 3:1: "This is now the second letter that I am writing to you, beloved." (ESV) The "you" in

this second letter is the same addressees of the first letter that Peter wrote. Who were these people? Note I Peter 1:1 which says: "Peter, an apostle of Jesus Christ, To those who are elect exiles of the Dispersion in Pontus, Galatia, Cappadocia, Asia, and Bithynia, …" (ESV) This word "Dispersion" in Greek is "diaspora" and this means Jewish believers in Jesus and the areas where they lived are herein identified.

We have noted that St. Paul wrote to the Jewish believers in the land of Israel and this letter identifies Jewish Christians living in areas around the Mediterranean in the First Century. Now look at what St. Peter said in this section of II Peter 3 and look how closely this links to the idea of the World to Come or the Millennial Age:

"In both of them I am stirring up your sincere mind by way of reminder, that you should remember the predictions of the holy prophets and the commandment of the Lord and Savior through your apostles, knowing this first of all, that scoffers will come in the last days with scoffing, following their own sinful desires. They will say, "Where is the promise of his coming? For ever since the fathers fell asleep, all things are continuing as they were from the beginning of creation." For they deliberately overlook this fact, that the heavens existed long ago, and the earth was formed out of water and through water by the word of God, and that by means of these the world that then existed was deluged with water and perished. But by the same word the heavens and earth that now exist are stored up for fire, being kept until the day of judgment and destruction of the ungodly.

But do not overlook this one fact, beloved, that with the Lord one day is as a thousand years, and a thousand years as one day. The Lord is not slow to fulfill his promise as some count slowness, but is patient toward you, not wishing that any should perish, but that all should reach repentance. But the day of the Lord will come like a thief, and then the heavens will pass away with a roar, and the heavenly bodies will be burned up and dissolved, and the earth and the works that are done on it will be exposed.

Since all these things are thus to be dissolved, what sort of people ought you to be in lives of holiness and godliness, waiting for and hastening the coming of the day of God, because of which the heavens will be set on fire and dissolved, and the heavenly bodies will melt as they burn! But according to his promise we are waiting for new heavens and a new earth in which righteousness dwells." (II Peter 3:2-13 ESV)

Notice how closely this is linked to what Paul talked about in Hebrews 4 saying:

"Therefore, while the promise of entering his rest still stands, let us fear lest any of you should seem to have failed to reach it. For good news came to us just as to them, but the message they heard did not benefit them, because they were not united by faith with those who listened. For we who have believed enter that rest, as he has said, "As I swore in my wrath, 'They shall not enter my rest,'" although his works were finished from the foundation of the world. For he has somewhere spoken of the seventh day in this way: "And God rested on the seventh day from all his works.

And again in this passage he said, "They shall not enter my rest."

Since therefore it remains for some to enter it, and those who formerly received the good news failed to enter because of disobedience, again he appoints a certain day, "Today," saying through David so long afterward, in the words already quoted,

"Today, if you hear his voice, do not harden your hearts."

For if Joshua had given them rest, God would not have spoken of another day later on. So then, there remains a Sabbath rest for the people of God, for whoever has entered God's rest has also rested from his works as God did from his." (Hebrews 4:1-10 ESV)

We've already noted the possibility that Peter is speaking about Paul's letter to the Hebrews in II Peter 3:15. Paul and Peter both are talking about a 1,000 year period, "a Sabbath rest". This follows up on what Moses said in Psalm 90:1-4, a special Psalm written by Moses:

"Lord, you have been our dwelling place in all generations. Before the mountains were brought forth, or ever you had formed the earth and the world, from everlasting to everlasting you are God. You return man to dust and say, "Return, O children of man!" For a thousand years in your sight are but as yesterday when it is past, or as a watch in the night." (ESV)

Both Paul and Peter began to realize in their lifetimes that our Lord Jesus was not coming back, but rather that there were many hundreds of years ahead of them before our Lord Jesus would return. Paul said that "there remains a Sabbath rest for the people of God" (Hebrews 4:10) which was definitely in the future to his time.

Following this section, we have Paul entering into a discussion about looking towards the example of the rebellious people from the 40 year period of the Exodus and the idea of a future Sabbath rest. We must remember that there was great expectation among Jewish believers in Jesus that the Messianic Age was soon to arrive on earth. Paul here reminds Jewish Christians about the rebellious generation in the wilderness and the 40 year period. Those people did not enter into the rest following the 40 year period and Paul may very well be reiterating to his target audience that the same was to be the case in the period of time after Jesus died in 30 AD up until the time of the Jewish Roman War in 70 AD. He tells his readers that the real Sabbath rest, which is a symbol of the Millennial Age, is something to come in the future.

Peter, in talking to the same target group, reiterates this idea in II Peter 3:1-13. Peter here gives an exhortation to the Jewish Christians (who Peter was the Apostle to) at his time telling them to be patient about the coming of the Lord. This passage is closely linked to what Paul is saying in Hebrews 3 and 4 about the Sabbath rest. This is because the Millennial Age was understood to be a 1,000 year period. The Sabbath[23] was a weekly reminder that this Millennial and Messianic Age was to come in the future, but Paul and Peter help to place this event into the future well after their times with the link to the seven day week cycle. This is because in the time of Jesus among Jewish believers, they came to believe more in a 7,000 year plan of God, which comprised a 6,000 year time for mankind on earth followed by a 1,000 year time period of the Kingdom of God on earth, known in Hebraic culture as "The Age to Come."

---

[23] The first point we have to understand about "work" is that we have to understand definitively what "work" is in the context of the Torah. This is where we can be assisted by the Hebrew scholars and sages who have been discussing and defining these issues for generations. "Work" is to be understood as a "purposeful act from which advantage is derived." Danby, Herbert: The Mishnah, Oxford University Press: Oxford, 1933, 1991. Pg. 111, foot note 6. (Therefore, on the Sabbath, no purposeful acts from which advantage is derived are permitted to be undertaken. This is not only the spirit of the day of the Sabbath, but it also the spirit of the Sabbath in the future, the Age to Come.

While the Sabbath was indeed a day that took place as the last actual day of each week, this day also had another significance. This was a typical teaching which pointed to a future time which was defined as 1,000 years in length and the seven (7) days of the week were typical of a 7,000 year period of human redemption: six (6) of those periods (or days) were designated for the "work" of man, whereas the seventh was a time where God and man were both to "rest."

The idea that days symbolically can typically refer to time periods of 1,000 year periods is a well-known Biblical one. Directly from the Biblical text we can point precisely to the following. Note first Psa. 90:3, 4.

"You return man to dust and say, "Return, O children of man!" For a thousand years in your sight are but as yesterday when it is past, or as a watch in the night. (Psalm 90:3-4 ESV)

Here we see the idea that a one thousand year period according to the way that God looks at things relates to a single day time period in the physical world.

In this same line of thinking, we have to add another Biblical text, which helps support our assertion here:

"Then I saw thrones, and seated on them were those to whom the authority to judge was committed. Also I saw the souls of those who had been beheaded for the testimony of Jesus and for the word of God, and those who had not worshiped the beast or its image and had not received its mark on their foreheads or their hands. They came to life and reigned with Christ for a thousand years. The rest of the dead did not come to life until the thousand years were ended. This is the first resurrection. Blessed and holy is the one who shares in the first resurrection! Over such the second death has no power, but they will be priests of God and of Christ, and they will reign with him for a thousand years." (Revelation 20:4-6 ESV)

Here we can see a connection of a 1,000 year time period obviously that takes place after the return of Jesus Christ back to this earth. These ideas were not new in the New Testament period. Peter, Paul and John (the author of Revelation) were not bringing up a totally new teaching which was unfamiliar to the first century audience. Not at all. In fact this idea of the Sabbath being symbolically associated with a 1,000 year period of time in the future (known as the Millennium or the 'Age to Come')

A specific textual testimony in this regard is found in the book of Jubilees, which was written at least 100-150 years before the birth of Jesus Christ. The book of Jubilees has as its subject matter generally the book of Genesis and it seeks to fill in some information from that book which is not clearly mentioned in Genesis itself. It offers a clear connection of a 1,000 year period as being connected to a single day.

"And at the close of the nineteenth jubilee, in the seventh week in the sixth year thereof, Adam died, and all his sons his sons buried him in the land of his creation, and he was the first to be buried in the earth. And he lacked seventy years of one thousand years; for one thousand years are as one day in the testimony of the heavens and therefore was it written concerning the tree of knowledge: "On the day that ye eat thereof ye will die." For this reason he did not complete the years of this day; for he died during it [before 1,000 years was completed]." (Jubilees 4:29,30)

In addition to this, we have the assertion from Philo Judaeus (20BC – 50AD), a writer from a Hebraic background from Alexandria, Egypt who mentioned that the length of human existence on earth would be 7,000 years.

This was stated in a way to show a link to the seven days of creation and that each day was symbolically linked to a 1,000 years period.

This idea continued through the New Testament period and is once again found in a very early Christian work known as the epistle of Barnabas. This reflects well the ideas which Peter and Paul began to understand and teach. Note what that author also said:

"Give heed, children, what this means; He ended in six days. He means this, that in six thousand years the Lord shall bring all things to an end; for the day with Him signifies a thousand years; and this He himself bears me witness, saying; Behold, the day of the Lord shall be as a thousand years. Therefore, children, in six days, that is in six thousand years, everything shall come to an end."[24] (Barnabas 15:4)

To summarize here, it is essential to understand the following:

1.   The Sabbath was the seventh day of the physical week and it was designed to be a day of rest where no work was undertaken
2.   The Sabbath was not only the seventh day of the physical week, but it was also symbolically associated with a 1,000 year period, known as the Millennium, which would commence with the return of Jesus Christ back to this earth.

---

[24] www.earlychristianwritings.com/text/barnabas-lightfoot.html - translated by J. B. Lightfoot

3.   This belief was well known and numerous ancient testimonies from Hebraic and Christian sources are in evidence (which we have referenced herein).

4.   The Seven Day Weekly Sabbath was a symbol of the "World to Come"

It was a well-known belief in the Second Temple period among Israelites that the Sabbath had a symbolic meaning associated with it. We can note this fact in the New Testament and in other texts at that time originating from Hebraic sources.

The primary symbolic meaning of the Sabbath was that it represented an experience on earth of what the future afterlife offered. Note the following quotes which refer to this.

In the Mishnah, one rabbi says, "This world is like a lobby before the Olam Ha-Ba (meaning "the age to come"). Prepare yourself in the lobby so that you may enter the banquet hall." (Pirke Avot 4:16) Another source shows the link between the World to Come and the Sabbath saying: "In the hour God said to Israel, "I am giving you the Torah," God said, "If you observing the mitzvah (commandment) of Shabbat, I will give you Olam Haba (the world to come)." And Israel said before God, "Master of the Universe! Show us an example of this Olam Haba." God replied, "This is Shabbat." (Midrash Otiot d'Rabbi Akiva)[25]

This idea that one day equaled 1,000 years echoes back to the first chapters of Genesis in which it was believed that humanity would have 6,000 years after which would follow a 1,000 year Sabbath period.

---

[25] https://www.sefaria.org.il/sheets/8314?lang=bi

We also find allusions to this in Hebrews in a very subtle way. We have noted earlier in this book that the main subject of the book of Hebrews is the Millennial Age (Hebrews 2:5), but notice the following text in Hebrews 1:1-2. If you are not in tune to the thinking and orientation of the writer, you may not consider this idea:

"Long ago, at many times and in many ways, God spoke to our fathers by the prophets, but in **these last days** he has spoken to us by his Son, whom he appointed the heir of all things, through whom also he created the world." (ESV)

If one were to look at this text, one could see a link to the Sabbath orientation for the 7,000 year plan of God. In one way of describing it, one could learn from the phrases "the former days," "the present days" and "these last days" to be describing three periods of 2,000 years each (totaling six days of 1,000 years each). It could be a subtle reference by St. Paul to the reader who was in tune with his message.

Conclusion

We have herein presented a case which seeks to better understand the whole of the book of Hebrews in its context. We have shown the importance of the position of Hebrews as the tenth letter of 14 in the Pauline collection and the idea that it follows II Thessalonians and the subject matter discussed in that book.

I think we can all agree that in the time when Paul wrote, it would not have been so easy to openly discuss matters related to the end of the age and the return of Jesus to this earth or even Jerusalem. However, to those people, to whom he wrote, they may have very well thought and

87

believed that Jesus would return in their lifetimes. Some of them may have been questioning the validity of our Lord's message and work because He had not returned yet or His return did not appear to be imminent. They may also at that time been suffering because of their belief in that idea.

We today know that Jesus still has not returned to earth and while we believe it will happen in the future, we have seen throughout history how negative it has been for Christians who began movements or put forward the idea that Jesus was returning to earth in their lifetimes. It could very well be that the subject of the book of Hebrews was presented to help reorient a community who was thinking the end of the age was soon to arrive.

8

Who is the book of Hebrews relevant for today?

In this research study, we are suggesting that the book of Hebrews was written to a specific group of people at a specific time for a specific reason. In that regard, we are suggesting the following:

1. The book of Hebrews was written to Hebrew Christians, that is, Jewish believers in our Lord Jesus Christ as the Messiah
2. The book of Hebrews was written to these believers who lived in the area of Jerusalem (or were intimately familiar with the geography of Jerusalem)
3. It was written in an environment of the mid to late First Century AD and is distinctive to that time
4. It was written or produced under the clear guidance of St. Paul the Apostle
5. The main subject focus of Hebrews is the Millennial Age to Come

In this book, we have focused on demonstrating the above mentioned facts. Now, we have to ask ourselves: Does the above point about the book of Hebrews being written to Hebrew Christians remain relevant today? After all, if it was written to Hebrew Christians in the past, does its relevance change today in light of the history over the last 2,000 years? This is an important question.

This, however, is not an easy question. In fact, it is a downright uncomfortable question. This is because the book of Hebrews is sacred scripture and Paul tells us that "all scripture is inspired." (II Timothy 3:16,17). It is inspired. How could it be that this book somehow does not have some universal, timeless applicability which many today seem to attach to it? Here we are entering into the field of systematic theology. We are asking you (and ourselves): "What is it that God wishes us to believe or not believe about the book of Hebrews? Is the thing that God wishes us to believe about this book different at all than other New Testament books? Let us consider this issue.

First, I think that all of us would agree that there are certain texts in the New Testament which are definitely not directed to all people universally. For example, we all remember the stories about the two instances in the Gospel of Luke (chapters 5 and 17) which speak about Jesus healing lepers. In one instance it was one person (ch.5) and in the other it was ten lepers. (ch.17)

Now my question to all of us is this. Is this story somehow relevant to Christians today? It is in the Bible. It is a part of Scripture and it is inspired, but I think that most people would say that this event is describing something that took place as a part of the ministry of Jesus Christ, but this does not have any real bearing on the practical Christian lives of Gentile Christians living outside of Israel today. Jesus even told the lepers "to go and show yourselves to the priests" which was required in the Law of Moses and Jesus also mentioned "giving an offering for your cleansing." (Luke 5:14) Now, most reasonable Christian people will point out that this took place under the Mosaic administration and that Christ had not yet died for the sins of the world and the Holy Spirit had not yet arrived. And they would be right! This information concerns something that took place at a particular time, under a particular religious administration which is no longer operating today and which has in fact been replaced for Christians today by the message of salvation through Christ alone.

Therefore, I think we can say that this text, while it is pure, holy and true, yet it is no longer really relevant for Christians in a practical sense today. What we see is that that story of the lepers in Luke is telling us the truth, but that truth was the truth for that time under those circumstances, but it is not necessarily the truth for us today. After all, there is no functioning priesthood operating at a Temple in Jerusalem today. The circumstances that governed that situation and that event have now changed and are no longer relevant as they were back then.

Not only do we see that truth can change over time, but also note that depending on the various circumstances at hand, there are two segments of truth operating at the same time among two different groups of people. That is a fact. Let us move down to a later time in the book of Acts and see this assertion demonstrated. Let us remember the situation that took place in the middle of the First Century in Jerusalem, when a dispute arose concerning the issue of circumcision. Let us review the text in question that says:

"But some men came down from Judea and were teaching the brothers, "Unless you are circumcised according to the custom of Moses, you cannot be saved." And after Paul and Barnabas had no small dissension and debate with them, Paul and Barnabas and some of the others were appointed to go up to Jerusalem to the apostles and the elders about this question. So, being sent on their way by the church, they passed through both Phoenicia and

Samaria, describing in detail the conversion of the Gentiles, and brought great joy to all the brothers. When they came to Jerusalem, they were welcomed by the church and the apostles and the elders, and they declared all that God had done with them. But some believers who belonged to the party of the Pharisees rose up and said, "It is necessary to circumcise them and to order them to keep the law of Moses." (Acts 15:1-5 ESV)

There were a group of Jewish believers in Jesus who had the truth. Their truth was that they were telling Gentiles that they needed to be circumcised and keep the Law of Moses even though they were believers in Jesus. That was the truth that they were advocating. And what happened?

"After they finished speaking, James replied, "Brothers, listen to me. Simeon has related how God first visited the Gentiles, to take from them a people for his name. And with this the words of the prophets agree, just as it is written,

"'After this I will return, and I will rebuild the tent of David that has fallen; I will rebuild its ruins, and I will restore it, that the remnant of mankind may seek the Lord,   and all the Gentiles who are called by my name, says the Lord, who makes these things known from of old.'

Therefore my judgment is that we should not trouble those of the Gentiles who turn to God, but should write to them to abstain from the things polluted by idols, and from sexual immorality, and from what has been strangled, and from blood. For from ancient generations Moses has had in every city those who proclaim him, for he is read every Sabbath in the synagogues." (Acts 15: 13-21 ESV)

So, a new truth was directed to Gentiles which was a type of compromise which was accepted at that time as an acceptable solution to allow for inter-group fellowship between Jewish Christians and Gentile Christians. But the important point here is that at no time were the original Jewish believers told to abandon their view and their adherence to the Law of Moses. They were allowed to continue practicing circumcision and keeping the Laws of Moses if they wished, but Gentile Christians were not required to do so. So, a divergence in the stream of truth was noted. A truth emerged for Jewish Christians that involved them continuing to keep the Laws of Moses, whereas Gentile Christians did not embrace the Laws of Moses including circumcision, but both worshipped the same God and both held a belief that Jesus was the Messiah and both had their respective truths for their own groups.

Later in the book of Acts we see the following mentioned about the Jewish Christians who were present in Jerusalem and the land of Israel saying:

"When we had come to Jerusalem, the brothers received us gladly. On the following day Paul went in with us to James, and all the elders were present. After greeting them, he related one by one the things that God had done among the Gentiles through his ministry. And when they heard it, they glorified God. And they said to him, "You see, brother, how many thousands there are among the Jews of those who have believed. **They are all zealous for the law,** (Acts 21:17-20 ESV)

This is not difficult to explain because Paul tells us in II Timothy 2:15 to:

93

"be diligent to present thyself approved to God -- a workman irreproachable, rightly dividing the word of the truth;" (Young's Literal Translation)

What we see in Acts is an exact example of this. The word of truth for two different groups was divided or partitioned into truth for one group and truth for the other group. Both were the truth to the respective party to whom that truth was directed at the time it was directed. It is important to note, however, that "all who have sinned under the law will be judged by the law." (Romans 2:12 ESV)

So, if the above suggestion holds true for individual texts or information directed to divergent groups in the New Testament, what about information found in whole books? Is it possible that information found in whole books in the New Testament is specifically designed for one group of people and not for another? In light of the above mentioned evidence, it seems a very reasonable question to ask and this is what we intend to ask now concerning the book of Hebrews and it is who its teachings are relevant for today.

The Book of Hebrews and its Target Group of Readers

The best place to analyze the relevance of the book of Hebrews and to whom it was directed is to look at the book itself and what it says. Let us notice the subject matter which will assist us greatly in our discussion.

First, Paul commences his discussion about the book of Hebrews about talking about angels. Note the comment from my late father about this issue where he says this:

"It is important to note that the first two chapters are devoted to showing the superiority of Christ over all angels. This was important for Paul to demonstrate because it was well recognized in the first century by the Jewish authorities that the Mosaic Law had been given to Israel through the agency of angels and Paul mentions this fact in Hebrews 2:2. Indeed, this present age (until the second advent of Christ) was reckoned as being in the charge of angels, both good and bad (Daniel 10:13-21; Matthew 4:8-10). But Paul, in the Book of Hebrews, was not going to discuss the kingdoms of this world during the time angels are in a limited control."[26]

What the text in Hebrews points to is the fact that it was well known in the first century that the Law of Moses was delivered to Moses by the hands of angelic powers. Note Josephus, the Jewish historian who said:

"We have learned the noblest of our doctrines and the holiest of our laws **from the angels** sent by God."[27]

This same idea is reiterated in Acts 7:53 where Saint Stephen said the following:

"Who have received the Law by the **disposition of Angels**, and have not kept it."

This is further mentioned by Paul in his letter to the Galatians, which says:

---

[26] Martin, Ernest L. Restoring the Original Bible: ASK Publications; Portland: OR, 1994. p.374
[27] Josephus, Antiquities of the Jews, XV, 5:3 Whiston

"Wherefore then serves the Law? It was added because of transgressions, till the seed should come to whom the promise was made, and it was **ordained by angels** in the hand of a mediator." (3:9)

Now considering this information, I think we can all agree that the section from Hebrews 1:1 to 2:18 is certainly inspired Scripture. However, one has to ask the question about its relevance for Christians today, especially believers who are not living in Israel and who are not observing the Law of Moses?

Gentile Christians who became believers in Jesus Christ never inherited or were taught a belief about the role of angels in the delivery of the Law of Moses to the people of Israel. They may have known about it, but this information had no real practical relevance to them. Why? We can see why in other texts given by Paul, like:

"For there is one God, and there is one mediator between God and men, the man Christ Jesus, who gave himself as a ransom for all, which is the testimony given at the proper time. For this I was appointed a preacher and an apostle (I am telling the truth, I am not lying), a teacher of the Gentiles in faith and truth. (I Timothy 2:5-7 ESV)

Here we see the teaching of Paul and his emphasis on his role as a teacher of the Gentiles and what he taught them. Paul taught the Gentiles that they had no mediators between themselves and God, except Jesus Christ. No angels, principalities, powers or any other force. Because of this, the question arrives. How relevant is Hebrews 1:1 to 2:18 to Gentiles?

Continuing in Hebrews 3:1-6, it says the following:

"Therefore, holy brothers, you who share in a heavenly calling, consider Jesus, the apostle and high priest of our confession, who was faithful to him who appointed him, just as Moses also was faithful in all God's house. For Jesus has been counted worthy of more glory than Moses—as much more glory as the builder of a house has more honor than the house itself. (For every house is built by someone, but the builder of all things is God.) Now Moses was faithful in all God's house as a servant, to testify to the things that were to be spoken later, but Christ is faithful over God's house as a son. And we are his house, if indeed we hold fast our confidence and our boasting in our hope."

When we read this text, we certainly appreciate its importance, but as Gentile believers in Jesus, how relevant is it to us in our understanding? Gentile believers never really grew up or were oriented to the importance of Moses as the giver of the Law of God. However, for Jewish Christians, this was not the case. Moses was the most important of all the saints in the Hebrew Bible. Really there is no more important person in the Jewish religion than Moses. But Paul says that Jesus is more important than Moses in the above referenced text. Gentile believers would not have needed to be reminded of this or taught this because they were taught about Jesus directly being the Messiah, the son of God. Yes, Jesus was like Moses in many ways because He fulfilled the role of the prophet mentioned in Deuteronomy 18: 1-5, but as Hebrews 3:2 tells us, Jesus was more important than Moses because He was the Son of God. Gentile Christians would never need to have this information reiterated to them because they were taught that in being introduced to Christianity and they had a personal connection directly to our Lord through the indwelling of the Holy Spirit. It was no longer God dwelling with you. It was now, God dwelling in you.

"Do you not know that you are a temple of God and that the Spirit of God dwells in you?" (I Corinthians 3:16 ESV)

This reiterates the exact teaching of Jesus, who said:

"And I will ask the Father, and he will give you another Helper, to be with you forever, even the Spirit of truth, whom the world cannot receive, because it neither sees him nor knows him. You know him, for he dwells with you and will be in you." (John 14:16,17 ESV)

This is how Gentile Christians were oriented towards God. They were not oriented towards spiritual powers, holy places, prophets and patriarchs, eating certain foods and observing certain days. They were oriented towards a teaching of:

"To them God chose to make known how great among the Gentiles are the riches of the glory of this mystery, which is **Christ in you**, the hope of glory." (Colossians 1:27 ESV)

Paul later says in Hebrews 13 the following:

"For here we have no lasting city, but we seek the city that is to come." (Hebrews 13:14 ESV)

This echoes very much the teaching of Jesus in the Gospel of John, which when John wrote his Gospel, this time had now arrived on earth.

Remember Jesus' conversation with the Samaritan woman and what he told her.

"Our fathers worshiped on this mountain, but you say that in Jerusalem is the place where people ought to worship." Jesus said to her, "Woman, believe me, the hour is coming when neither on this mountain nor in Jerusalem will you worship the Father. You worship what you do not know; we worship what we know, for salvation is from the Jews. But the hour is coming, **and is now here**, when the true worshipers will worship the Father in spirit and truth, for the Father is seeking such people to worship him. God is spirit, and those who worship him must worship in spirit and truth." (John 4: 20-24 ESV)

Gentile Christians would never have needed to have been told this because they were coming to faith, receiving the Holy Spirit and practicing the fruits of that Holy Spirit and joining the family of God as sons, not going through any other processes. The experience for Jewish Christians was different than this and this is why we see it mentioned here in Hebrews 3.

Just after this section, Peter also says to the same Jewish Christians the following about Paul:

"Therefore, beloved, since you are waiting for these, be diligent to be found by him without spot or blemish, and at peace. And count the patience of our Lord as salvation, just as our beloved brother Paul also wrote to you according to the wisdom given him, as he does in all his letters when he speaks in them of these matters. There are some things in them that are hard to understand, which the ignorant and unstable twist to their own destruction, as they do the other Scriptures. You therefore, beloved, knowing this beforehand, take care that you are not carried away with the error of lawless people and lose your own stability. But grow in the grace and knowledge of our Lord and Savior Jesus Christ." (II Peter 3:14-18 ESV)

We have already seen that there is a strong likelihood that the Jewish Christians to whom Peter was addressing may have been familiar with or heard about Paul's teachings to the Hebrews.

After this, you have a lengthy discussion by Paul in Hebrews 3:6-4:13 dealing with the future rest, how the Sabbath was a shadow of the future. The point is though concerning this discussion, it only exhibits a relevance for those keeping the Sabbath or wishing to understand the symbolism of the Sabbath related to the future Millennial Age. It is not really relevant for believers today who are not keeping the Sabbath.

Notice also the section of Hebrews from 4:13 to 5:10. This discussion is not really relevant to Christians today. It only makes sense in a context where the recipients of the letter would be more familiar with a religious system which had a High Priest in operation. Such was not the case for Gentile believers.

The Voice in Hebrews – Who is Talking and Who is Listening?

In our study of the book of Hebrews, we really need to look at the evidence that allows us to arrive at certain conclusions. This includes looking at the whole of the text itself as well as its place among the other letters of Paul. This evidence is going to help us later to address other issues especially surrounding the matter of corporal punishment/spanking/smacking and the text of Hebrews 12:5-11.

Before we do that, however, let us consider the matter of voice in Hebrews and how listening, looking and paying close attention to the issue of voice in the text is essential to better understand Hebrews. What we are talking about is not only the voice of the writer or writers, but also the voice of the audience. If our assertion in this book is that this book is directed to Jewish Christians, then the voice in the text should have evidence available that contributes to this view or hopefully demonstrates this clearly. I think that when we look at these data, we will find this to be the case.

This analysis is very powerful and full of evidence from which we can extract quite a lot of practical information. This study involves a careful examination of the pronouns used in the text and the information associated with those pronouns and what it says which help us to better understand not only the issue of voice in the text, but also contributes to a better understanding of who the text is relevant for and how we can better interpret the information making sure we are applying this information to the right target group.

To best do this, a thorough discussion is needed to capture the richness of the material. What needs consideration is the individual and collaborative voices in the text. First, let's look at the individual voice because as we have noted in this book, St. Paul wrote Hebrews. The individual voice of the main writer of the book is found in Hebrews 11:32 saying:

"And what more shall I say? For time would fail me to tell of Gideon, Barak, Samson, Jephthah, of David and Samuel and the prophets ..."

101

Here we seem to have a very direct reference to a single author. This is in direct contrast to some of Paul's other writings which definitely have multiple writers taking part such as the following letters:

"Paul, Silvanus, and Timothy, To the church of the Thessalonians in God the Father and the Lord Jesus Christ: Grace to you and peace. We give thanks to God always for all of you, constantly mentioning you in our prayers ..." (I Thessalonians 1:1-2 ESV)

"Paul, Silvanus, and Timothy, To the church of the Thessalonians in God our Father and the Lord Jesus Christ: Grace to you and peace from God our Father and the Lord Jesus Christ. We ought always to give thanks to God for you, brothers, as is right, because your faith is growing abundantly, and the love of every one of you for one another is increasing." (II Thessalonians 1:1-4 ESV)

We see in the letters to the Thessalonians a bit of a rarity when it comes to ancient letter writing. According to the late Father Jerome Murphy O'Connor, he notes that most instances of multiple authors in ancient letters are rare.[28] This gives us a stronger indication that the letter to the Hebrews is written by a single person.

This is not without controversy though because the Greek language of Hebrews is a very high level of Greek and because of this many scholars have said that it could not be Paul writing it. There is no problem with this issue because by the time that Paul would have written Hebrews, he could very well have had someone else transcribe it or to wholly

---

[28] Jerome Murphy-O'Connor, *Paul the Letter-Writer: His World, His Options, His Skills* (Good News Studies, Vol. 41; Collegeville, MN: The Liturgical Press, 1995), pp. 16-19

compose it based on his instructions. As we note from my earlier timeline chart, Paul probably lived to be at least 70 years of age. Some have said that maybe Paul also had eye problems which affected his sight. We do know he said:

"What then has become of your blessedness? For I testify to you that, if possible, you would have gouged out your eyes and given them to me." (Galatians 4:15 ESV)

There is also this text which depending on how one looked at it could lend itself to the idea that St. Paul did not see very well:

"And looking intently at the council, Paul said, "Brothers, I have lived my life before God in all good conscience up to this day." And the high priest Ananias commanded those who stood by him to strike him on the mouth. Then Paul said to him, "God is going to strike you, you whitewashed wall! Are you sitting to judge me according to the law, and yet contrary to the law you order me to be struck?" Those who stood by said, "Would you revile God's high priest?" And Paul said, "I did not know, brothers, that he was the high priest, for it is written, 'You shall not speak evil of a ruler of your people.'" (Acts 23:1-5 ESV)

There is also the simple fact that once Paul was also stoned and left for dead:

"But Jews came from Antioch and Iconium, and having persuaded the crowds, they stoned Paul and dragged him out of the city, supposing that he was dead. 20 But when the disciples gathered about him, he rose up and entered the city, and on the next day he went on with Barnabas to Derbe." (Acts 14:19-20 ESV)

Paul also mentioned that he had some type of "thorn in the flesh" which he pleaded to God to take away and God refused to take it away. Let us refer to this text:

"So to keep me from becoming conceited because of the surpassing greatness of the revelations, a thorn was given me in the flesh, a messenger of Satan to harass me, to keep me from becoming conceited. Three times I pleaded with the Lord about this, that it should leave me. But he said to me, "My grace is sufficient for you, for my power is made perfect in weakness." Therefore I will boast all the more gladly of my weaknesses, so that the power of Christ may rest upon me." (II Corinthians 12:7-9 ESV)

This thorn in the flesh could be related to damage to his eyes due to being stoned as mentioned in Acts 14. Some of these other texts seem to support that idea. In any case, it is quite possible that Paul could have dictated the letter to someone else who composed it for him as a secretary. See Appendix II concerning this issue.

Timothy is mentioned in the text of Hebrews and was a direct apprentice of the Apostle Paul. Timothy started his apprenticeship with Paul probably sometime after turning 13 or perhaps a little older, so by the mid 60's, Timothy would still perhaps not yet have reached 30 years of age because we find Paul telling Timothy the following:

"Let no one despise you for your youth, but set the believers an example in speech, in conduct, in love, in faith, in purity." (I Timothy 4:12 ESV)

This was probably composed in the mid-60's so it is quite conceivable that Timothy at this time had not yet reached 30 years of age, after which he would almost certainly not have been described as a "youth."

Further Considerations Relative to Voice in Hebrews

What we want to do now is to look at the text of the book of Hebrews more in detail and see these facts demonstrated.

To begin, let us start with Hebrews 1:1, which says:

"Long ago, at many times and in many ways, God spoke to our fathers by the prophets ..." (ESV)

Now, in looking at this text we can immediately note that the people in question are identified as "our fathers" that "God spoke to" "by the prophets."

What we see in this text is a very clear reference to the Jewish people who received divine communication through many prophets going back to the time of Abraham in particular, but more fully with Moses and the later prophets.

We see certain terminology which was commonly used by Jewish people when they were communicating one with other. Not the following examples of this in the book of Hebrews saying:

"Therefore, holy **brothers**, you who share in a heavenly calling ..." (3:1 ESV)

"Take care, **brothers**, lest there be in any of you an evil, unbelieving heart, leading you to fall away from the living God." (3:12 ESV)

"Therefore, **brothers**, since we have confidence to enter the holy places by the blood of Jesus…" (10:19 ESV)

"I appeal to you, **brothers**, bear with my word of exhortation, for I have written to you briefly. You should know that our **brother** Timothy has been released, with whom I shall see you if he comes soon." (13:22,23 ESV)

Commenting on this issue, Claire Pfann, Academic Dean (www.uhl.ac), notes that:

"1. In Acts 1-9, ἀδελφός, (*adelphos* - "brother") is applied only to Jews. They can be Jews by birth or converts to Judaism. They may or may not believe in Jesus as the Messiah. If they are Jewish, they are of Abraham and thus, brothers."[29]

Continuing. Note once again Hebrews 1:1, which starts out by saying:

"Long ago, at many times and in many ways, God spoke to our fathers by the prophets …"

---

[29] Pfann, Claire – Comments on "brother" in Acts – "Who is my Brother?" Course – Acts of the Apostles – University of the Holy Land – www.uhl.ac. "The first time adelphos is used with reference to a Gentile is in 15:1 (there an exception to draw the attention of the audience to the narrative), and then from Acts 15:23 and throughout the rest of Acts, Luke uses it freely to refer to Jews who don't believe in Jesus, Jews who do believe in Jesus and Gentiles who believe in Jesus." – www.uhl.ac.

Now, this starts to define the target group who is being addressed in the book of Hebrews. It says that "God spoke to our fathers by the prophets." What we see in this text seemingly is a clear statement that I think we can all agree with.

1. When the writer says "our fathers" he is identifying himself as a Jewish Christian person, and he is also speaking to a group of Jewish Christian people through the text. This is especially relevant in light of the fact that this book is addressed "To Hebrews" who are believing that Jesus is the Messiah.

2. Who is the God in question? The Almighty God, who created heaven and earth and who is revealed in the Hebrew Bible. There is no doubt about this from the rest of the book of Hebrews.

3. The prophets in question are clearly the Hebrew prophets mentioned in the Hebrew Bible.

I think we can all agree that the voice in the text is clearly a learned Jewish Christian person/people addressing other Jewish Christian people. At this point, we are not able to demonstrate that they are Christians, but that will come shortly. Let's now consider some more identifying pronouns to help us really identify who are the writers as well as the readers.

Note the following texts from the book of Hebrews:

Texts	Quotations all from the English Standard Version (ESV)
1:2	"but in these last days he has spoken **to us** by his Son …"
2:1	"Therefore **we** must pay much closer attention …"
2:1	"to what **we** have heard …"
2:1	"lest **we** drift away from it."
2:3	"how shall **we** escape …"
2:3	"if **we** neglect such a great salvation?"
2:3	"and it was attested **to us** by those who heard …"
2:8	"At present, **we** do not yet see everything in subjection to him."

2:9	"But **we** see him who for a little while was made lower than the angels ..."
2:16	"For surely it is not angels that he helps, but he helps **the offspring of Abraham.**"

Reading all of this first section makes a clear ending connection in 2:16 to the offspring of Abraham. It is hard to be any clearer that this is the target group in question. What we can see in this group of texts is a very clear plural voice. The writer or writers are making it clear that they are a part of the target group themselves. Hebrews is full of this type of usage and I believe we need to pay attention to this.

In addition, however, paying attention to the plural pronouns in the book of Hebrews offers us some very interesting teachings. This issue concerns quite a number of texts, but it is important to review the evidence and perhaps form that we can make some assertions in support of our suggestions herein.

What we are going to see over and over again is the emphasis on the Hebrew Christian context, on Jerusalem but with some small beginnings of leadings away from the Law of Moses more into the realm of grace. This is very much where Paul had gone with his letters to the Gentiles, but to his brethren, the Jewish Christians, he took a slower pace and took as his basis the Law of Moses and their orientation to it in these assertions and we see lots of evidence for that in the book of Hebrews. Without question, the words "we" and "our" in these texts are NOT addressing all believers at all. This letter is directed to a specific group and the voice of the text demonstrates that.

Let us continue our review of the voice and plural pronouns in Hebrews:

Texts	Quotations all from the English Standard Version (ESV)
3:12	"Therefore, holy **brothers and sisters**"
3:6	"**we** are his house, if indeed **we** hold fast **our** confidence and **our** boasting in **our** hope."
3:12	"Take care, **brothers**, lest there be in any of **you** an evil, unbelieving heart, leading **you** to fall away from the living God."
3:13	"But exhort one another every day, as long as it is called "today," that none of **you** may be hardened by the deceitfulness of sin."
3:14	"For **we** have come to share in Christ, if indeed **we** hold our original confidence firm to the end."
3:19	"So **we** see that they were unable to enter because of unbelief."
4:1	"Therefore, while the promise of entering his rest still stands, let **us** fear lest any of **you** should seem to have failed to reach it."
4:2	"For good news came to **us** just as to them, but the message they heard did not benefit them, because they were not united by faith with those who listened."
4:3	"For **we** who have believed enter that rest …"
4:11	"Let **us** therefore strive to enter that rest, so that no one may fall by the same sort of disobedience."
4:14	"Since then **we** have a great high priest who has passed through the heavens, Jesus, the Son of God, let **us** hold fast our confession."
4:15	"For **we** do not have a high priest who is unable to sympathize with **our** weaknesses, but one who in every respect has been tempted as **we** are, yet without sin."
4:16	"Let **us** then with confidence draw near to the throne of grace, that **we** may receive mercy and find grace to help in time of need."
5:11	"About this **we** have much to say, and it is hard to explain, since **you** have become dull of hearing."
5:12	"For though by this time **you** ought to be teachers, **you** need someone to teach **you** again the basic principles of the oracles of God. **You** need milk, not solid food,"
6:1	"Therefore let **us** leave the elementary doctrine of Christ and go on to maturity …"
6:3	"And this **we** will do if God permits."
6:9	"**we** speak in this way, yet in **your** case, beloved, **we** feel sure of better things"
6:10	"For God is not unjust so as to overlook **your** work and the love that **you** have shown for his name in serving the saints, as **you** still do."

When we continue reviewing the voice in these texts, we see it does not change and remains consistent talking to and about the same target group: Hebrew Christians.

Texts	Quotations all from the English Standard Version (ESV)
6:18	"**we** who have fled for refuge might have strong encouragement to hold fast to the hope set before **us**."
6:19	"**We** have this as a sure and steadfast anchor of the soul, …"
6:20	"where Jesus has gone as a forerunner on **our** behalf, …"
7:19	"a better hope is introduced, through which **we** draw near to God."
7:26	"For it was indeed fitting that **we** should have such a high priest,"
8:1	"Now the point in what **we** are saying is this: **we** have such a high priest, …"
9:5	"Of these things **we** cannot now speak in detail."
10:21	"and since **we** have a great priest over the house of God, …"
10:22	"let **us** draw near with a true heart in full assurance of faith, with **our** hearts sprinkled clean from an evil conscience and **our** bodies washed with pure water."
10:23	"Let **us** hold fast the confession of our hope without wavering, …"
10:24	"And let **us** consider how to stir up one another to love and good works,"
10:26	"For if **we** go on sinning deliberately after receiving the knowledge of the truth,"
10:29	"How much worse punishment, do **you** think, will be deserved by the one who has trampled underfoot the Son of God, …"
10:30	"For **we** know him who said"
10:32	"But recall the former days when, after **you** were enlightened, **you** endured a hard struggle with sufferings, …"
10:34	"For **you** had compassion on those in prison, and **you** joyfully accepted the plundering of **your** property, since **you** knew that **you yourselves** had a better possession and an abiding one."
10:35	"Therefore do not throw away **your** confidence, which has a great reward."
10:36	"For **you** have need of endurance, so that when **you** have done the will of God **you** may receive what is promised."
10:39	"But **we** are not of those who shrink back and are destroyed, but of **those** who have faith and preserve their souls."
11:2	"For by it **the people of old** (or "**our ancestors**") received their commendation."
11:3	"By faith **we** understand that the universe was created by the word of God, …"

What we notice about this letter is the continued unbroken narrative and very communal nature of the discussion. It is very much the writer joining with the recipients. The point in this exercise is to show that the book of Hebrews is a text written by a Hebrew scholar (Paul) to a Hebrew community in the land of Israel talking about their situation and their need to remain connected to our Lord Jesus. The text has complete unity and it is not possible to somehow say that this text has a more universal orientation like the Gospel of John, for example. It is important that we understand that the words "we, you and us" in this text do not include Christians today living outside of a Hebraic context in the land of Israel.

Let us finalize our review of the voice and the plural pronouns in Hebrews:

Texts	Quotations all from the English Standard Version (ESV)
11:32	"And what more shall **I** say? For time would fail **me** ..."
11:37	"**They** were stoned, **they** were sawn in two, **they** were killed with the sword. **They** went about in skins of sheep and goats, destitute, afflicted, mistreated—"
12:1	"**we** are surrounded by so great a cloud of witnesses, let **us** also lay aside every weight, and sin which clings so closely, and let **us** run with endurance the race that is set before **us**,"
12:3	"Consider him ... , so that **you** may not grow weary or fainthearted."
12:4	"And have **you** forgotten the exhortation that addresses **you** as sons?"
12:7	"It is for discipline that **you** have to endure. God is treating **you** as sons."
12:9	"Besides this, **we** have had earthly fathers who disciplined **us** and **we** respected them. Shall **we** not much more be subject to the Father of spirits and live?"
12:10	"For they disciplined **us** for a short time as it seemed best to them, but he disciplines **us** for **our** good, that **we** may share his holiness."
12:14	"Strive for peace with **everyone**,"
12:18	"For **you** have not come to what may be touched, a blazing fire and darkness and gloom and a tempest and the sound of a trumpet and a voice whose words made the hearers beg that no further messages be spoken to them. For they could not endure the order that was given, "If even a beast touches the mountain, it shall be stoned." Indeed, so terrifying was the sight that Moses said, "I tremble with fear.""
12:22	"But **you** have come to Mount Zion and to the city of the living God, the heavenly Jerusalem, and to innumerable angels in festal gathering,"
12:25	"See that **you** do not refuse him who is speaking. For if they did not

	escape when they refused him who warned them on earth, much less will we escape if **we** reject him who warns from heaven."
12:28	"Therefore let **us** be grateful for receiving a kingdom that cannot be shaken, and thus let **us** offer to God acceptable worship, with reverence and awe,"
12:29	"for **our** God is a consuming fire."
13:6	"So **we** can confidently say, "The Lord is my helper; I will not fear; what can man do to me?" (Quoting here Psalm 118:6)
13:7	"Remember **your** leaders, those who spoke to **you** the word of God. Consider the outcome of **their** way of life, and imitate **their** faith."
13:9	"Don't be led away by diverse and strange teachings, ... be strengthened by grace, **not by foods**, which haven't benefited **those** devoted to **them**."
13:10	"**We** have an altar from which those who serve the tent have no right to eat."
13:13	"Therefore let **us** go to him outside the camp and bear the reproach he endured."
13:14	"For here **we** have no lasting city, but **we** seek the city that is to come."
13:15	"Through him then let **us** continually offer up a sacrifice of praise to God,"
13:16	"Do not neglect to do good and to share what **you** have,"
13:17	"Obey **your** leaders and submit to them, for they are keeping watch over **your** souls,"
13:19	"I urge **you** the more earnestly to do this in order that I may be restored to **you** ... ."
13:21	"equip **you** with everything good that **you** may do his will, working in **us** ..."
13:22-25	"I appeal to **you, brothers** ... I have written to **you** ... . **You** should know that **our brother** Timothy has been released, ... I shall see **you** ... Greet all **your** leaders and all the saints. Those who come from Italy send **you** greetings. Grace be with all of **you**.

In Hebrews 11:32, we see the writer revealing a single author overall in the text, while later on he will say also to "pray for us." (13:18) This would seem to indicate Paul mentioning Timothy whom he mentions by name in 13:23.

What this last section exhibits is further evidence which reiterates our main point herein that this community of Hebrew Christians living in the land of Israel are still retaining some of the elements of Judaism in their faith walk. There is a direct reference in 12:18 of the original transmission of the Law of Moses to the people of Israel. While Paul does indeed mention this, he is not remiss to remind the Hebrew Christians in 12:22 about a "heavenly Mount Zion" coupled with the advice in 13:13 and 13:14 to go outside of the camp of Israel to that altar (the cross of our Lord Jesus) and a new city which is to come.

The key point in all of this discussion is that it is not possible to separate this text from the original recipients and their presence and situation is ever present in the reading. This is what makes applying this material to "Christians" in general mistaken. It does serious violence to the text and misapplies material which is clearly destined for one group of Christians (Hebrew Christians living in the land of Israel and in particular the city of Jerusalem before 70 AD) to another group (Gentile Christians living outside of Israel after 70 AD) to whom it was never directed towards.

9

How does this survey of Hebrews link to our understanding of the debate concerning spanking children in the 21st century?

In this book, I have attempted to lay a good foundation to actually try to develop a greater understanding of this text:

"And have you forgotten the exhortation that addresses you as sons?

"My son, do not regard lightly the discipline of the Lord,
    nor be weary when reproved by him.
For the Lord disciplines the one he loves,
    and chastises every son whom he receives."

It is for discipline that you have to endure. God is treating you as sons. For what son is there whom his father does not discipline? If you are left without discipline, in which all have participated, then you are illegitimate children and not sons. Besides this, we have had earthly fathers who disciplined us and we respected them. Shall we not much more be subject to the Father of spirits and live? For they disciplined us for a short time as it seemed best to them, but he disciplines us for our good, that we may share his holiness. For the moment all discipline seems painful rather than pleasant, but later it yields the peaceful fruit of righteousness to those who have been trained by it. (Hebrews 12:5-11 ESV)

We have concluded the following concerning the messages of the book of Hebrews:

1. It was written to Hebrew Christians living near Jerusalem before 70 AD.
2. It was written by St. Paul. (or certainly under his guidance)
3. It contains teachings which are given for a particular group of people, for a particular reason in a particular circumstance.
4. It contains an overall message seeking to show the recipients that our Lord Jesus Christ would not be returning from heaven in the immediate future as many of the recipients thought.

This represents the main points we have addressed so far in this book, but now we must directly focus on a really hard question: Is this text applicable today to Christians in general or was it directed to a particular group at a particular time for a particular reason which today is no longer relevant? This is what we want to know.

Christians have been asking hard questions
about Hebrews for centuries

Many of the questions that we have raised in this book about certain texts in Hebrews have been asked for centuries and Christians have been (and continue to be) troubled by certain texts in Hebrews. Hebrews 12:5-11 is one of these texts which causes much consternation with many Christian families.

Christians have had questions about Hebrews for centuries because its teachings are confusing for them. Earlier in this book, we noted the following texts:

- Hebrews and its supposed advocacy of corporal punishment (12:5-11)
- Hebrews and its supposed advocacy of tithing for Christians (7:2-10)
- Hebrews' supposed advocacy and demand for church attendance (10:25)
- Hebrews' demand that all Christians "Obey your leaders" (13:7)
- All of these teachings are wrapped up with Hebrews 6:4-8 and 10:26-35, which say:

"For it is impossible, in the case of those who have once been enlightened, who have tasted the heavenly gift, and have shared in the Holy Spirit, and have tasted the goodness of the word of God and the powers of the age to come, and then have fallen away, to restore them again to repentance, since they are crucifying once again the Son of God to their own harm and holding him up to contempt. For land that has drunk the rain that often falls on it, and produces a crop useful to those for whose sake it is cultivated, receives a blessing from God. But if it bears thorns and thistles, it is worthless and near to being cursed, and its end is to be burned." (ESV)

"For if we go on sinning deliberately after receiving the knowledge of the truth, there no longer remains a sacrifice for sins, but a fearful expectation of judgment, and a fury of fire that will consume the adversaries. Anyone who has set aside the law of Moses dies without mercy on the evidence of two or three witnesses. How much worse punishment, do you think, will be deserved by the one who has trampled underfoot the Son of God, and has profaned the blood of the covenant by which he was sanctified, and has outraged the Spirit of grace? For we know him who said, "Vengeance is mine; I will repay." And again, "The Lord will judge his people." It is a fearful thing to fall into the hands of the living God.

But recall the former days when, after you were enlightened, you endured a hard struggle with sufferings, sometimes being publicly exposed to reproach and affliction, and sometimes being partners with those so treated. For you had compassion on those in prison, and you joyfully accepted the plundering of your property, since you knew that you yourselves had a better possession and an abiding one. Therefore do not throw away your confidence, which has a great reward." (ESV)

As mentioned before, these are key texts used to threaten Christians that if they do not listen and heed the words of this book as interpreted by many misguided pastors, they are going fall under the curses listed here and will be placed in the category of "**impossible … to renew them again unto repentance**" and "**It is a fearful thing to fall into the hands of the living God.**" I reiterate that these texts connected together engender immense fear in many God fearing believers. Basically, many Christians feel that these texts teach that they can lose their salvation in Christ if they don't follow these teachings. As was mentioned, one can see the "imprisonment" nature of the theology. Coupling these texts together can create this horrible cocktail of fear and being imprisoned by the very Word of God.

As I said these fears are not new. What we can say though is that these questions have been brought more out in the open in the last 400 years as the Bible has become much more accessible in Western society, particularly in the English speaking world. This is certainly good, but in environments where there is freedom of religion or the separation of church and state and the practice of Christian faith is unregulated by any authorities, the Bible can be used in a way as described above and Christian brothers and sisters may feel trapped by religious leaders using these kinds of teachings.

A great example of a group of people who were considering these questions is found about 125 years ago in England. During this time, there was a renewed interest in the Bible during this time to counter the introduction of the Theory of Evolution in 1859. Christian education in England in particular was going very well concerning the Bible. Christian publishing and teaching was very active and had been slowly improving over the previous few hundred years. The Industrial Revolution was in full swing and Christians also we starting to take part in pilgrimages to Israel, so Bible education was advancing.

During this period, however, much confusion existed surrounding some of these very teachings we are herein addressing concerning Hebrews. In particular as noted was Hebrews 6:3-8 and 10:26-35. These texts scared some Christians and they found them confusing. Many Christian brothers and sisters feared for their eternal souls on the basis of these texts and what they seemed to teach on the surface.

This matter is discussed at length by the late English Bible Scholar, Dr. E. W. Bullinger. Dr. Bullinger was an active Bible scholar and writer who produced a huge body of work through a journal called "Things to Come" that he served as the editor for some 28 years before his death in

1913. Dr. Bullinger is also well known for the Companion Bible, for which he served as the chief editor and for several other books. Dr. Bullinger was also a very conservative Bible believer who very carefully studied the Biblical texts.

It is through Dr. Bullinger's writings that we know about this issue of Christian fear in England about 125 years ago surrounding the book of Hebrews. Dr. Bullinger saw the situation and the danger of it and thankfully chose to address this matter at that time no doubt to the full satisfaction of many who read his wonderful explanations. We today can also benefit from this tireless servant of God who toiled over Holy Writ during a very active Bible teaching ministry.

Dr. E. W. Bullinger, Dispensationalism and the
Epistle to the Hebrews

Through the Journal "Things to Come", Dr. Bullinger published an article in February 1901, pg. 98, titled: "The Epistle to the Hebrews." We are here going to refer extensively to this important article.

First, Dr. Bullinger notes that he had previously published his ideas about Hebrews and the necessity to understand the teaching of dispensationalism relative to that book and its place in the Bible saying:

"We have already indicated what we believe to be the dispensational place and position of the Epistle to the Hebrews. But it is necessary to speak of this more fully, inasmuch as the failure to notice this is the cause of great trouble to many of the children of God." (pg.98)

He lamented the situation he found in England among many Christians he knew in his time who were very troubled over the book of

119

Hebrews and as such, he felt an absolute demand to respond to this situation which he ably did through this article.

What he means here concerning dispensationalism is that God has revealed Himself to mankind through the Word of God in stages, each time revealing more and more of Himself and His teachings.

We can understand it like this. Starting with Adam and Eve, God revealed very few instructions and information. Later, with Abraham, we had more information and revelation given. Later on with Moses, more information was given and the five books of Moses were written down. As time went on, God continued to reveal more information to King David and the Prophets. Then, the period of the Old Testament closed.

Then, Jesus was born and grew up and started to preach. He revealed a message, which was later augmented after His death and then by the giving of the Holy Spirit and the teachings of the Apostles starting in Jerusalem and then those teachings given by St. Paul which stretched out to the whole world.

My late father used the term "**progressive revelation**" to describe how God gave His truths to mankind. He described it very much like what St. Paul said in Galatians talking about the Law of Moses as a "schoolmaster to lead people to Christ." (Galatians 3:24) What St. Paul used was a kind of a school system illustration and we can understand the Bible and its teachings in the same way. Notice this explanation from a booklet where he describes the teaching of "**progressive revelation**."

"Let us first understand the intent of the phrase. By "progressive" we do not mean "modern" or "liberal." We are using it in the sense of something being passed successively from one point of a series to the next. Or, even more definitely, "to progress step-by-step towards improvement until a desired higher plane of development is reached."

The principle is well attested in several biblical verses.

"But grow in grace, and in the knowledge of our Lord and Savior Jesus Christ" (Il Peter 3:18 KJV).

"That ye might walk worthy of the Lord unto all pleasing, being fruitful in every good work, and increasing in the knowledge of God" (Colossians 1:10 KJV).

"The path of the just is as a shining light, that shineth more and more unto the perfect day" (Proverbs 4:18 KJV)."[30]

Those of us who have children know that the teachings given in kindergarden are the truth for kindergarden attending children, but when you move out of kindergarden, those teachings, which were the truth for you at that time, have no further relevance. You have now matured into new truths. This is progressive revelation and it moves to grade school, secondary school, high school, college, grad school, post graduate work and even in some cases post-doctoral work. The teachings at each stage are really relevant for those who are under that system. This is what St. Paul was teaching in Galatians 3:24.

Dispensationalism (another word for "progressive revelation") teaches that God gave His truth slowly, in stages, step by step and what we need to understand is to orient ourselves into the correct dispensation for

---

[30] Martin, Ernest L. Progressive Revelation, FBR: Pasadena, CA: 1980 - Introduction

121

us. If we do this, we will have God's understanding for us. If we don't do this, we may be mixing teachings that God intended for others into what He intended for us and that would be mistaken.

This is what Dr. Bullinger was pointing out some 125 years ago in this article about the book of Hebrews. This is what he saw taking place among Christians in England at that time. Some Christians were mixing teachings intended for one group or dispensation with another group or dispensation and this in the view of Dr. Bullinger was mistaken and lead to error.

Dr. Bullinger gets directly to the point in this article. People around him were raising serious questions about the book of Hebrews. He begins by showing the problem and then identifies exactly the reason for this problem saying:

"The number of questions put to us with regard to the falling away mentioned in Heb. 6:3-8, and the "no more sacrifice for sins," &c., in Heb. 10-26-35, show the seriousness of the difficulty which is created through not seeing the scope of the Epistle and not "rightly dividing the word of truth." (*ibid.*)

This issue of "rightly dividing the word of truth" (in reference, of course, to II Timothy 2:15) was essential to Dr. Bullinger and we who are aware of his writings know this was a key point for him as is the case normally for those following a more dispensationalist point of view in how the interpret Scripture.

Dr. Bullinger did point out in his opinion these texts created serious problems, but those problems had nothing to do with the texts themselves. Note what he said in this regard:

"That there is a problem (concerning interpretations of Hebrews 6:3-8 and 10-25-36) is certain: and it is a great one (as remains the case to this day). But it is entirely of our own creation. There is no difficulty whatever in the Epistle itself." (*ibid.*)

That is correct. It was correct then and it is still correct today. There is no problem with the book of Hebrews, with its texts or any information it contains. The problem that existed concerning Hebrews then is, unfortunately, exactly the same problem that exists today. What is that problem? We can note the assertion of Dr. Bullinger here:

"It (the problem discussed in the last quote) arises only because of our willful, selfish persistence in reading "The Church" into every part of the word of God. Many, while repudiating the title of 'Churchmen' with reference to the Historic church, are most devout 'Churchmen' with regard to the Bible hence the difficulty." (*ibid.*)

What we find Dr. Bullinger saying is that this problem concerning misunderstandings related to opinions introduced by religious leaders which were problematic. Unfortunately, we find the same thing happening today. The problem back then remains today. It is a problem of mistaken interpretation of the book of Hebrews and a misapplication of its teachings to the wrong people by religious authorities.

Dr. Bullinger continues this train of thought with a wonderful and empowering interpretation which we all need to let sink in and believe. We who love God's Word need to have tools to help us understand the book of books. In this regard, Dr. Bullinger has done a wonderful service to the Body of Christ.

He begins with a very powerful interpretive tool using the teaching our Lord gave about marriage to show how important it is to keep those things God has joined together or connected properly joined together.

"What ... God hath joined together, let not man put asunder" (Mark 10:9). These words are true; and they express an eternal principle, which teaches in its application far beyond the interpretation which confines them to the marriage tie." (*ibid.*)

What Dr. Bullinger is showing is that God has a design for things and this design, going back to II Timothy 2:15 quoted before, even affects the issue of truth and the Word of God. Continuing:

"But the converse is, and must be, equally true: *That which God hath put asunder, let not man join together.*" (*ibid.*)

This is a powerful statement and it is full of truth as we will see and it goes back again and again to this issue of "rightly dividing the word of truth." When man puts things together which God has designed to be separated, error will be the result. This can be the case even in our understanding of God's most precious Word. Continuing:

"This eternal truth (*That which God hath put asunder, let not man join together*) cannot be violated without loss and disaster; whether it be in our practical life, or in our reading and interpretation of the Word of God." (*ibid.*)

Here, to Dr. Bullinger, we have the crux of the problem. Things which should not be joined together or interpreted together are being done so, mistakenly by churchmen. It was happening in Dr. Bullinger's day and it is still happening today. Let's see a practical example of this by Dr. Bullinger now which concerns the book of Hebrews and how this book should be "separated" or "put asunder" from other Biblical books.

"God has "put asunder" for example, the Epistle to the Romans and the Epistle to the Hebrews. He might have corrected or incorporated the two in some way, if it had pleased Him to do so: but He has put them entirely "asunder," in fact and in form. And it is by joining these together we suffer harm and loss, and fall into the fatal snare **of using one truth to upset another truth**." (*ibid.*)

Herein lies the problem that Christians in the past had with Hebrews and its teachings compared to other teachings in the New Testament or in other letters of Paul. It was the problem they had back then and it is the problem we still have today.

I think we can all agree today that it is very common to find Christian ministers and Bible authorities writing about Hebrews and mixing its teachings from all over St. Paul's other epistles as if that is perfectly fine and the right thing to do from a Bible interpretation point of view. Dr. Bullinger will have nothing of the sort when it comes to doing such things with the Word of God. To him, doing this is "**using one truth to upset another truth**", which he calls a "**fatal snare.**" (*ibid.*)

Dr. Bullinger considers this approach to Bible interpretation a serious error. Note what he says in this regard concerning two different true documents:

125

"A statement may be perfectly true of the persons addressed, and of the time and occasion, & c., to which it specifically refers. Another statement, elsewhere, may also be perfectly true in the same way. But, if we join them together, and interpret them of the same persons, and of the same circumstances, all truth vanishes, and we have a great difficulty at once created, if not a direct contradiction." (*ibid.*)

This describes very well the situation that we Christians find ourselves in when it comes to the book of Hebrews and especially chapter 12:5-11. If we are interpreting it in the same way with all of the other letters of Paul, Dr. Bullinger says that is a huge mistake and he is right! He further demonstrates this using several Biblical texts saying:

"Take an example from Deut. 6:25: 'It shall be our righteousness, if we observe to do all these commandments before the LORD our God, as he hath commanded us.' These words are perfectly true as spoken to certain persons and at a certain time. But we read in Galatians 2:16: 'By the words of the law shall no flesh be justified.' These words also are perfectly true under another dispensation. Deuteronomy 6:25 is true of those under the covenant of *works*, and Galatians 2:16 is equally true of those who are under the covenant of *grace*. If they are thus put and kept 'asunder' all is perfectly clear; but if they are joined together, then the saint may well be perplexed, and the enemy of God's Word has a weapon put into his hand to use against all truth." (*ibid.*)

This situation described above describes, unfortunately, the Christian experience that many have today and the book of Hebrews is the "weapon of choice." Many people that I have communicated with over the years find some of these teachings very hard to accept. The precious Word of God has become a tool of control concerning:

- Hebrews and its supposed advocacy of corporal punishment (12:5-11)
- Hebrews and its supposed advocacy of tithing for Christians (7:2-10)
- Hebrews supposed advocacy and demand for church attendance (10:25)
- Hebrews demands that all Christians "Obey your leaders" (13:7)

All of these teachings are wrapped up with Hebrews 6:4-8 and 10:26-35. The question is though, as Dr. Bullinger reminds us, do we understand properly or are we "perplexed?" Are we joining something from one part of the Bible together with other Bible teachings which were never designed to be joined together with something else in the first place? This is what we have to ask ourselves. Note another example:

"We may take another illustration, which will bring us at once to the point before us. I may have a letter put into my hands, which I *assume* is written *to me*. I read on, and find much that is intensely interesting, and exceedingly profitable *for* me. But I find also references to matters which do not concern me. Things are said about my position which do not quite describe it. There may be a reference to a debt which I do not owe, or to an order which I do not remember having given. Persons and events are mentioned: but, not knowing exactly to whom or to what they refer, there is much that puzzles and perplexes me.

But all the difficulty is removed when I discover, and understand, that though the letter is put into my hand on purpose FOR me to read and learn, it was not actually addressed TO me." (*ibid.*)

This is important teaching, which we who love the Word of God need to heed. We need to "rightly divide the word of truth." We need to make sure we have a correct understanding of Scripture or the most beautiful thing God has given to us (outside of our Lord Jesus Himself), His Holy Word, can become a tool of imprisonment. This is especially the case when it comes to the issue of corporal punishment that we are addressing here in this book because this is one teaching that is mentioned in the book of Hebrews. If we don't do this, we are going to continue to be "perplexed" as Dr. Bullinger put it, but if we "rightly divide the word of truth" then:

"Then it all is clear. I quite see how I may profit by much of the instruction that is contained in the letter; and I am no longer troubled by that which seemed so different from another letter which the same writer had previously addressed directly *to me*, and which was all ABOUT me."

This is beautiful teaching. Why? It is because Hebrews is troubling for us in many ways. We read in other sections of Paul epistles statements seeming to be much more gentle, but what happens? Some Christians force us to home in on Hebrews because that is what the Bible says. It is a constant "Yes, but what about Hebrews 12:5-11" argument? Here is a great example of this that I received from a mother talking about the issue of spanking children and you can see how troubling and perplexing the whole issue was for her (before reading my first book in this series – which is free for download here – www.biblechild.com):

"My husband and I have both read your free ebook but we would love to have a hard copy as well. Thank you for all of your work and study. I have always felt that spanking was wrong, but being surrounded by Christians who all spank, I was really second guessing myself and was having a hard time convincing my husband. I had read a few different interpretations of the proverbs "spanking" texts but none of them really held water. After we read your book, we no longer have doubts and feel fully confident in our decision to not spank. I wish we had come across your book the first time we were "talked to" about spanking. Now we are unified, prepared and confident in our decision and it feels good. Let me know how to go about purchasing your book. Thank you!!" (anonymous by request - personal testimony used with permission)

Now, this testimony shows clearly exactly what Dr. Bullinger is demonstrating. It is this tension between error and truth. It shows a deep personal desire to be right with God. It is the fear that surrounds us based on what the people around us are doing and what Christian religious authorities, our church families and our own families are demanding from us. It is the troubling perplexing problem that many Christians face surrounding some teachings in the Bible which are being promoted all around them, especially related to things like parenting. Sisters and brothers in Christ feel so out of step, so afraid, so uncertain. When they question these teachings, they are forced to second guess themselves. They begin to think that something is wrong with them. How crazy making this is, but thanks be to God, this dear sister and her husband were delivered from this error and have found a real substantive peace in the truth.

What we find is that much consternation and trouble exists in the minds of Christian brethren over the book of Hebrews. But this need not be. Dr. Bullinger continues talking about these two hypothetical letters and now brings in a direct comparison to Hebrews for our edification:

"Now this is exactly the case with the Epistle to the Hebrews. It is written 'FOR our learning', but it is not addressed TO us." (*ibid.*)

This is so powerful and simple and it is what I came to see in my own research in the last 6-12 months. People who have been following my work since I've been getting material ready for this book will agree with my assertion that I have been talking about this idea for some months now. Dr. Bullinger continues talking about Hebrews and to whom it is addressed:

"It is addressed to Hebrews (not Gentile Christians) at a particular time, under certain circumstances, and in a certain condition of mind. The *interpretation* therefore belongs exclusively to them; while the *application* belongs to all Christians in all time." (*ibid.*)

This is exactly the teaching that needs to be widely heard today about the book of Hebrews. These hodgepodge, mixed-up, thrown together teachings promoted as Biblical truth need to be jettisoned and we need to get back to the truth of God. We need to get back to OUR truth in OUR context, not THEIR truth in THEIR context.

Bullinger elaborates on an important point: the condition of mind of the recipients of the letter to the Hebrews. We have raised some ideas in this book, but Bullinger makes clear some key information about the target group for the Epistle to the Hebrews.

"These Hebrews and their spiritual condition we find described in Acts 21:20-26. They are the thousands who believed on and after the day of Pentecost. … Those Pentecostal (referring to those who were converted on the Day of Pentecost) believers, who are the ideal of many Gentile Christians today, were Hebrews who receive the Lord Jesus as the Messiah, … When Paul reached Jerusalem, in Acts 21:17, he met the Apostles and Elders in council, and they uttered these weighty, memorable words to Paul: *'Thou seest, brother, how many thousands of Jews there are which believe:' and they are all zealous of the Law.*" (Acts 21:20) (*ibid.*)

This is the target group we have been talking about in this book: Jewish believers in Messiah Jesus, who were "zealous of the Law." We have also identified them as being focused in the land of Israel and even around or especially knowledgeable of the city of Jerusalem.

We need to understand that Jewish believers in Messiah Jesus who were zealous of the Law and residing in the land of Israel, were in a much more conservative religious and a highly regulated environment. Keeping the law, practiced circumcision, keeping the feasts, keeping kosher food regulations, keeping the weekly Sabbath and the seventh year land Sabbath, paying the annual half-shekel temple tax, following the Mosaic rules, travelling to Jerusalem three times per year, these laws were all much higher profile events in the life and society of Israel in the time of Jesus and Paul. Paul calls himself a "Pharisee of the Pharisees" which is like saying: I am a conservative of the conservatives. His Phariseeism was being practiced at a very high and rigorous level. Living in the land of Israel meant that one was in general practicing a much more conservative practice of Judaism than those Jewish believers who lived outside of Israel.

This issue extended into all areas of life even affecting the issue of corporal punishment/spanking/smacking as I have shown in my first book in this series (available for free download here – www.biblechild.com or on Amazon in hard copy). See the chapter: "The legal context of the book of Proverbs." We must understand the more rigorous nature of the faith practice that these believers were a part of living in the land of Israel. We know that corporal punishment was a part of the Law of Moses and even Paul himself mentions that he was subject to it five times as an adult. (II Cor. 11:24) Young men, not small children, who were moving to adulthood may have been subject to this by their fathers according to the teachings found in Proverbs.

In addition, we must also understand the gender implications of the book of Proverbs, which is decidedly oriented to young men, not small children or girls! The original texts in Proverbs just will not allow for including girls. See the first and fourth chapters of my book Thy Rod and Thy Staff, They Comfort Me; Christians and the Spanking Controversy (download it free – www.biblechild.com), which are: "The Phases of Child Development outlined in the Bible" and "The gender focus of the book of Proverbs."

Bullinger continues saying more about the people to whom Hebrews was sent:

"We are concerned with the Pentecostal Jewish believers; and it is clear that they were so "zealous of the Law" that they had not forsaken Moses, nor given up circumcision, but walked after the customs. Moreover, they offered sacrifices (verse 26) ..." (ibid.)

This, of course, is something that we who are Gentile believers cannot really appreciate because it is not a part of our faith background or experience at all. Having said this, however, for these believers it was totally normal and made perfect sense from a Biblical practice point of view.[31]

When we understand the beliefs, practices and circumstances of these Jewish believers in Christ who were soon expecting the Messianic Age to arrive, we are in a much better position to understand the book of Hebrews. Dr. Bullinger points this out exactly:

"To such the Epistle to the Hebrews would come with all its truth and power. Even we ourselves can understand it better if we look at the Epistle in this light. We can see exactly why the various arguments are used, and why all the many references to the Law are made. We can distinguish what is written FOR us: and not confound it with what is written TO us in the Epistle to the Romans." (*ibid.*)

This is beautiful teaching because it is true and it helps us rightly position Hebrews in its rightful place, which for those of us who are Gentile believers, it falls outside of our systematic theology. It is written **FOR** us, but not **TO** us.

Dr. Bullinger reminds us of our position "in Christ" as referenced in the book of Romans saying:

---

[31] Please see Appendix One for more information on this point. Note also: As we have mentioned that Paul's subject of Hebrews concerns the Age to Come or the Millennium, it would have made perfect sense for any God fearing community that thought that the Millennium was soon to arrive living in the land of Israel and keeping the Law of Moses to practice a rigorous approach to Judaism. This is because they would have had numerous texts in the Hebrew Bible indicating that after Jesus Christ returns, the Law of Moses is going to be reinstituted here on this earth. See Zechariah 14 and Isaiah 66.

"There (in Romans) we learn our position as having died with Christ, been buried with Christ, and risen with Christ. There we learn how there is "therefore no condemnation to them that are in Christ (Romans 8:1), and no separation from the love of God which is in Christ."

And learning all this, as a blessed fact written to and of ourselves, we shall never again be upset at what is written to others; or use what is truth, as written to them, to upset what is equally truth, as written to us. In other words, **we shall not use one truth to upset another truth. ...**" (*ibid.*)

Bullinger continues showing to whom Hebrews 6 and 10 are meant. It is to those who are:

"zealous of the Law," then Heb. 6 and 10 are meant and are true for you, and the sooner you take those scriptures to heart the better! But, for you who are in "Christ,", and know your standing "in Him," we exhort you to rejoice in all that is written to you as to your completeness and perfection in Christ Jesus our Lord." (*ibid.*)

To conclude, Dr. Bullinger reminds us (with some of the finest expositorial Bible teaching found anywhere) as Paul was also reminding those to whom he wrote that:

"the key-note of the Epistle is "better;" and Hebrew believers are shown how that "in Christ" they have everything "better" than under the Law of which they were so "zealous."

They had:

A better covenant (Hebrews 7:22)

Better promises (Hebrews 8:6)

Better substance (Hebrews 10:14)

A better hope (Hebrews 7:19)

A better sacrifice (Hebrews 9:23)

A better country (Hebrews 11:16)

A better resurrection (Hebrews 11:35)

A better thing (Hebrews 11:40)

Not only is the word "better" used, but Christ is shown to be:

Better than angels (Hebrews 1)

Better than Moses (Hebrews 3)

Better than Joshua (Hebrews 4)

Better than Aaron (Hebrews 7)

Better than the Law (Hebrews 10) (*ibid.*)

To this list, I will add that Jesus Christ is:

Better than the Sabbath (Hebrews 4)

Better than the future Rest (the Millennial Age to Come) (Heb. 4)

Better than Baptisms (Hebrews 6)

Better than Tithing (Hebrews 7)

Better than Corporal Punishment (Hebrews 12)

Better than the Old Earthly City (Hebrews 13)

Better than the Old Altar in the Temple (Hebrews 13)

We can find our place in Hebrews at an altar which was positioned outside of the camp, outside of the city, the altar which represents the true altar for us, where our Lord Jesus suffered and died for us. This is our altar and this is where we as Gentile Christians meet our Jewish Christian brethren. Our altar is the cross of our Lord Jesus. This is written to the Hebrews Christians in Jerusalem at that time, but this altar is the altar for the whole world, for all Christendom and it is mentioned in Hebrews:

"**We have an altar,** whereof they have no right to eat that serve the tabernacle. For the bodies of those beasts whose blood is brought into the holy place by the high priest as an offering for sin, are burned without the camp. Wherefore Jesus also, that he might sanctify the people through his own blood, suffered without the gate. **Let us therefore go forth unto him** without the camp, bearing his reproach. **For we have not here an abiding city, but we seek after the city (see John 4:23) which is to come.** Through him then let us offer up a sacrifice of praise to God continually, that is, the fruit of lips which make confession to his name." (Hebrews 13:10-15 ASV)

Where is our new city? In the heavenlies as St. Paul reminds us:

"If then ye were raised together with Christ, **seek the things that are above,** where Christ is, seated on the right hand of God. **Set your mind on the things that are above, not on the things that are upon the earth.** For ye died, and your life is hid with Christ in God. When Christ, *who is* our life, shall be manifested, then shall ye also with him be manifested in glory.

Put to death therefore your members which are upon the earth: fornication, uncleanness, passion, evil desire, and covetousness, which is idolatry; for which things' sake cometh the wrath of God upon the sons of disobedience: wherein ye also once walked, when ye lived in these things; but now do ye also put them all away: anger, wrath, malice, railing, shameful speaking out of your mouth: lie not one to another; seeing that ye have **put off the old man with his doings,** and have **put on the new man,** that is being renewed unto knowledge after the image of him that created him: where there cannot be Greek and Jew, circumcision and uncircumcision, barbarian, Scythian, bondman, freeman; but Christ is all, and in all.

Put on therefore, as God's elect, holy and beloved, **a heart of compassion, kindness, lowliness, meekness, longsuffering; forbearing one another, and forgiving each other,** if any man have a complaint against any; even as the Lord forgave you, so also do ye: and **above all these things** *put on* **love,** which is the bond of perfectness. And **let the peace of Christ rule in your hearts,** to the which also ye were called in one body; and be ye thankful. **Let the word of Christ dwell in you richly;** in all wisdom teaching and admonishing one another with psalms *and* hymns *and* spiritual songs, singing with grace in your hearts unto God. And whatsoever ye do, in word or in deed, *do* all in the name of the Lord Jesus, giving thanks to God the Father through him." (Colossians 3:1-17 ASV)

This is something that all of us who are parents need to remind ourselves of and this is why for many corporal punishment never feels right, because it is something that we as Christian believers in Christ have grown out of.

137

We must remember that when we read this, St. Paul taught us to:

"Be imitators of me, as I am of Christ." (I Corinthians 11:1 ESV)

Jesus is gentle and we should also strive to be gentle to be like Him. (Matt. 11:28-30)

Dr. Bullinger continues:

"Another word which characterizes this Epistle is the word "once"; i.e. once for all. (see 6:4; 7:27; 9:7, 12, 26, 27, 28; 10:2, 10; 12:26, 27.)

The Epistle is written to those who knew the Law. Hence they are exhorted in various ways:

"Let us" fear (4:1); labour (4:11); hold fast (3:6; 4:14; 10:23); come boldly (4:16); go on (6:1); draw near (10:22); consider (10:24); lay aside (12:1); run (12:1); have grace (12:28; go forth (13:13); offer (13:15).
Paul is trying through this approach to bring the readers of this Epistle to a new state of mind, a new way of thinking.

"The great design is to get them to break away from the traditional teaching to which they clung with such religious zeal. It has waxed old, and was about to vanish away (8:13). The Levitical Law and all its ordinances were among the "things that are shaken ... that those things which cannot be shaken may remain. (12:26-28).

All had failed. The Law: 'for the Law made nothing perfect" (7:19). It was characterized by 'weakness and unprofitableness" (7:18). (*ibid.*)

This is what our Lord Jesus through St. Paul is calling us mature Christians to: a new way of thinking dominated by the fruits of the Holy Spirit. (Galatians 5:22,23)

Here Dr. Bullinger is talking about the Law in that time. He would have been the first to acknowledge that after Jesus Christ returns, it will be reinstituted for those on earth at that time. But for those people back there in the land of Israel who were zealous for the Law, he says:

"According to chap. 6:1, 2, all these things were 'dead works.' It was necessary to 'go on unto perfection.' (6:1, *maturity* would express the Greek better); and to those who were minded thus to "go on" it is said, 'Beloved, we are persuaded better things of YOU' (6:9). (*ibid.*)

Paul then reorients the reader to where their true attention needs to focus at all times:

"Christ is the one object for faith in this Epistle. He supersedes all else. To look *for* Him (9:28) and to look *to* Him (12:2) is the substance of which all beside was only shadow.

To cling to traditions or to religion, as such, is to give up both these positions. It is this that gives all its importance to the climax which is reached in chap. 13, which is the great lesson on THE CAMP." (*ibid.*)

As shown earlier in our discussion in this book about the camp, we have seen that this issue of "the camp" found in Hebrews 13 points to an altar where our Lord Jesus was crucified and to Him outside the city, away from the Temple and away from the Law is where all people need to go. This is our true destination, an altar outside the camp.

Yet, in this present day, we still find people still mixing up Biblical teachings designed for one group of people with another and remaining focused on religion and tradition. Paul will have none of this:

"Hence, this Epistle has a very powerful *application* to thousands of professed 'believers' in the present day (Dr. Bullinger was writing in 1901, but his statement remains as true in 2019 as it was back then); an application as powerful as its *interpretation*, which came to those thousands of Jewish Christians who were 'all zealous of the law.' All who now are merely religious; holding by tradition; relying on ordinances; depending on rites and ceremonies, priests and sacraments, all these need the special lesson of this Epistle today; and to all such its *application* comes with overwhelming force, as powerful as its *interpretation* came at the first to those of the Jewish believers who were zealous of the law.

But those who have gone forth 'without the camp' know their completeness in Christ, read their standing in the Epistle to the Romans, and know that in Him there is 'no condemnation, ' and from Him there can be no separation." (*ibid.*)

This affirmative teaching of our Lord given through Paul, who spoke to both Jews and Gentiles (Acts 9:15) reminds us of the importance of rightly dividing the Word of Truth so that we are "workmen who do not need to be ashamed." (II Timothy 2:15) So, we who are Gentiles take and learn from this material in Hebrews knowing that it is FOR us, but not TO us and we do so with absolute confidence that we have the true message of God in our hearts and minds. Let us hear what St. Paul said to us.

What is this true message for us? It is a message of peace and reconciliation. It is a message of grace, not law. It is a message of reality, not shadows of things to come. It is a message of friendship. It is a gentle message from a loving God. As we have seen in this book, this text from Hebrews is NOT written to Gentile Christians. It has an orientation which comes directly out of an adherence to the Law of Moses.

This is where it is important that we learn to:

"be diligent to present thyself approved to God -- a workman irreproachable, rightly dividing the word of the truth;" (II Timothy 2:15) (Young's Literal Translation)

We must discern what texts are **"to us"** directly and what texts are **"for us"** generally. This will help us to remain steadfast in the truth that God has provided to us and helps ensure that we do not overturn one truth with another.

The book of Hebrews in its original context and how we can understand it

The analysis of Dr. Bullinger overall is very helpful. Now we can get down to a more detailed consideration of some of the key points in Hebrews, which directly cause many parents in particular consternation relative to the issue of corporal punishment/spanking/smacking.

Before we do that, let us also consider some explanations of why some of these other points[32] are found in the book of Hebrews and how those issues were relevant for the Hebrew Christians in the land of Israel that the book was written to, but are not relevant for us today. We've

---

[32] Hebrews and its supposed advocacy of corporal punishment (12:5-11); Hebrews and its supposed advocacy of tithing for Christians (7:2-10); Hebrews supposed advocacy and demand for church attendance (10:25); Hebrews demand that all Christians "Obey your leaders" (13:7)

discussed the issue of tithing already, but what about the text in Hebrews (10:25) which seems to urge church attendance?

We have put forward the thesis in this book that Hebrews has an orientation towards a community of people whose expectation of the arrival of the Messianic Age was very high. In this environment, people would be undertaking preparations for that event and those preparations could involve isolating oneself and one's family away from society. Anyone who reads the Bible's texts related to the coming of the "Day of the Lord" are well aware of the cataclysmic descriptions that are found in many of the Old Testament books, which this community would have been acutely aware of.

Paul mentioned this because he knew some of the community in Israel who were Hebrew Christians were then resorting to this behavior due to their expectation that the Messianic Age was soon to arrive. The idea of isolating one's self and family is even found in Scripture. Notice the following text from Isaiah, which is strongly linked to the time of the coming of the Day of the Lord, saying:

"Come, my people, enter your chambers, and shut your doors behind you; hide yourselves for a little while until the fury has passed by." (Isaiah 26:20 ESV)

I think the situation and context that the recipients of this letter to the Hebrews demands that we pay attention to that situation, who the people were and what they circumstances were which suggested mentioning this issue. Without question, this text has no relevance to demand that modern Christians to attend church services.

It is also interesting that Paul mentions the issue of some not holding a positive or restrictive view of marriage (Hebrews 13:4) at that time. This is especially unusual for a Hebraic oriented community who were "zealous for the law" (Acts 21:20), which had as the first commandment in the Law of Moses to "be fruitful and multiply." (Genesis 1:28) One can better understand the relevance of mentioning this point about the holiness and sanctity of marriage in light of a community who thought the Messianic Age was soon to appear. A community had to have a very specific reason for seeking to delay or restrict marriage. The pressure and stress on the community at that time may have dictated it, but Paul tells them that marriage was honorable and to be respected by all (Hebrews 13:4).

It is also important to note the issue of "Obey your leaders." (Hebrews 13:7) This point has a totally different meaning in a context where the recipients are a Hebraic oriented, Torah observant society that believed that Jesus was the Christ, which would have had the God ordained hierarchical leadership structure found in the Aaronic priesthood and the family of the Levites as well as those individuals who were members of the family of King David, from which our Lord descended in the flesh.

Those groups of people in a Hebraic context would have had a God given, inalienable right of leadership among the community which would have been recognized and respected. The leaders of the Christian community in Israel at Jerusalem, who were Jewish believers in Jesus, had some association to these families.

The principle of eldership which was a cross-cutting issue for the society would also have been in evidence there in Israel and Jerusalem at that time.

First, we have even the family of our Lord Jesus Himself, of which two persons who wrote books in the New Testament are mentioned: James and Jude (Jacob and Judah in Hebrew). Both of them were, of course, from the family of David according to the flesh.

Second, you have the Apostle John, who wrote five books in the New Testament (his Gospel, the three epistles and Revelation). He was the son of Salome and Zebedee. Salome was the sister of the Mary, the mother of our Lord Jesus. Mary was the relative of Elizabeth, the mother of John the Baptist (who was an Aaronic priest). So, the Apostle John would also have been an Aaronic priest. This fact would have afforded him a rank in the society as a priest of the line of Aaron, which would have been an ascribed status which would have afforded him a leadership role.

What we must realize is that many of the first leaders of the Christian community in Israel and Jerusalem were relatives of our Lord Jesus in a physical sense being a part of the same family and having Mary as their mother.

I think it imperative that we consider these matters relative to the text in Hebrews 13:7. To remove that text outside of its original context and transport it into some modern application is in my view a serious error in Biblical interpretation.

Finally, concerning the issue of corporal punishment/spanking/smacking, I have discussed at length in my first book the essential fact that we must understand that this information in Hebrews is directly linked to a more rigorous adherence to the Law of Moses. In the land of Israel, the practice of Judaism and keeping the Law of Moses was much more conservative. Because of that, shame versus honor would be operating in the society at a much higher level and the necessity of younger men to adhere to these strong societal rules would have been very high. A young man who was without proper behavior could find himself in a very serious situation where the influence of his extended family could not help him due to inappropriate, life threatening actions. In this environment, we find the issue of corporal punishment /spanking/smacking from a paternal point of view directed towards boys mentioned as it was part of Mosaic Law.

This information though, was and is not directed to Gentile Christians, who were not under the Law of Moses, were not raised with it or required to keep it and were urged to pursue the fruits of the Holy Spirit (5:22,23).

Conclusion

In my first book, *Thy Rod and Thy Staff, They Comfort Me: Christians and the Spanking Controversy*, I developed a thesis about an orientation found in the book of Proverbs which is linked very much to the Law of Moses. I tried to show that this orientation is not binding today on Christians who are not under the Law of Moses. All of the teaching material in Proverbs has that orientation as its basis and as such, we Christians today, need to take this fact into consideration in reading and applying Proverbs rightly.

The exact same situation is the case in regard to reading and understanding the book of Hebrews. This is especially the case today because it involves something so important as corporal punishment directed towards children. I pray we can all read Scripture in a way that leads us toward peace and not away from it, so help us God.

Let us see how Christians today can reach a mature level of progressive revelation. The mature message of God to Christian parents is summarized as follows:

145

Central Teaching of God as Found in the New Testament following a "*To us*" approach rightly dividing the word of truth for mature Christians found below.
"Come to me, all who labor and are heavy laden, and I will give you rest. Take my yoke upon you, and learn from me, **for I am gentle and lowly in heart**, and you will find rest for your souls. For my yoke is easy, and my burden is light." Matt. 11:28-30
"But the hour is coming, *and is now here*, when the true worshipers will worship the Father in spirit and truth, for the Father is seeking such people to worship him." (John 4:23)
I no longer call you servants, because a servant does not know his master's business. Instead, **I have called you friends**, for everything that I learned from my Father I have made known to you. (John 15:15 NIV)
Recompense to **no man evil for evil**. Provide things honest in the sight of all men. If it be possible, as much as lieth in you, **live peaceably with all men**. Dearly beloved, avenge not yourselves, but rather give place unto wrath: for it is written, Vengeance is mine; I will repay, saith the Lord. Therefore if thine enemy hunger, feed him; if he thirst, give him drink: for in so doing thou shalt heap coals of fire on his head. **Be not overcome of evil, but overcome evil with good**. - Romans 12:17-21
But the fruit of the Spirit is love, joy, peace, patience, kindness, goodness, faithfulness, gentleness, self-control; **against such things there is no law**. (Gal. 5:22, 23 ESV)
"What do you want? Shall I come to you with a rod, **or in love and a spirit of gentleness?**" (I Corinthians 4:21 NKJV)
"And the fathers! **provoke not your children**, but nourish them in the instruction and admonition of the Lord." (Ephesians 6:4 YLT)
"Therefore, as the elect of God, holy and beloved, **put on tender mercies, kindness, humility, meekness, longsuffering**; bearing with one another, and forgiving one another," (Colossians 3:12,13 NKJV)
"**Fathers, do not provoke your children, lest they become discouraged.**" Colossians 3:21 NKJV)
"These things have I spoken unto you, that **my joy may be in you, and that your joy may be made full**. This is my commandment, **that ye love one another, even as I have loved you. Greater love hath no man than this, that a man lay down his life for his friends**." (John 15:11-13 ASV)

146

APPENDIX I

My personal experience with tithing and further linkages to the issue of corporal punishment/spanking/smacking

First of all, I can state unequivocally that I do not tithe and I don't believe that tithing is binding on Christians at all. I happen to take this matter very seriously and even personally because I have seen and learned firsthand the damage and rotten spiritual fruit that this false teaching of tithing has yielded in the lives of 1,000s of God-fearing Christian people. The teaching of tithing as presented today is false. There are far too many Christian pastors today who would do a lot better as leaders if they followed the example of Jesus, who was a poor man who walked around Israel in poverty, to heart.

Tithing, as you can tell, is no small issue with me. It was no small issue also with my late father, so much so that he wrote several books about the subject of tithing. His work on tithing began as a pamphlet of some 40+ pages called, "*The Tithing Fallacy*." That little pamphlet had a wonderful impact. It was reprinted many times reaching more than 100,000 copies in print. Later, this pamphlet was revised and a new more updated longer version in book form came into being called, "*The Tithing Dilemma*."

My late father had a very specific reason for writing those books on tithing. This was because in 1974, he voluntarily left a former association he had with the Worldwide Church of God, where he held senior executive and ministerial roles, which taught one of the more aggressive tithing doctrines of any church I have ever encountered. They also taught one of the most aggressive forms of corporal punishment/spanking/smacking that I have encountered in my 25+ years of studying this issue.

The Worldwide Church of God was a fairly large Sabbath keeping denomination which held to a Christian belief which included some elements of Judaism. Those elements included keeping the Jewish festivals (opposed to Christmas and Easter), not eating certain foods based on Jewish law and definitely keeping the Sabbath. This church practiced an aggressive form of tithing which included false teachings associated with second and third tithes, which are mentioned in the Bible, however, the leaders of the World Wide Church of God twisted these teachings around and used them to aggressively raise money from their church members. Church members often lived in poverty to adhere to these false teachings. In addition to tithing, the church had an aggressive form of soliciting offerings on top of tithes, so many people in the church were further impoverished due to these teachings. To add insult to injury, the main leader of the church was one of the first televangelists to have his own private Learjet and flew around the world in luxury meeting political leaders.

In response to his negative experience in the church, my late father took it upon himself after leaving the denomination to begin to publish openly on a variety of Biblical subjects and tithing was one of the first subjects he addressed due to the urgency surrounding this issue. It is important also to remember that in 1974, the USA was facing very serious

148

economic problems and many of the people he knew were suffering and were hurt by the aggressive teaching of tithing being promoted by the Worldwide Church of God at that time. These are the main points that my late father raised on tithing which are still as relevant as when they were first brought out in 1974.

I urge anyone interested in this subject to follow up on this issue through the following link.[33] The main findings of the book can be summarized as follows:

1. Jewish people today do not tithe as mentioned in the Bible to finance their religious activities.

2. Tithing was only applicable generally speaking to the Land of Israel.[34] Some other lands like Babylonia later became "tithable",

---

[33] http://www.askelm.com/tithing/index.asp
[34] **Tithing Only For the Land of Israel -** Another factor that has often been overlooked concerning the biblical tithing system is the fact that it only applied to those Israelites who lived in Israel.

"And all the tithe *of the land,* **whether of the seed** *of the land,* **or of the fruit of the tree, is the Lord's: it is holy unto the Lord."** *Leviticus 27:30*

Notice a major point about this tithing instruction. It said **"All the tithe of the land ... is the Lord's."** This Hebrew word rendered "land" is *aretz.* At times the word can mean the earth (Genesis 1:1). At other times it is used with regard to a specific land or country (Exodus 3:8, 17). Many times the term, as used in Leviticus 27:30, refers specifically to the land of Israel in Palestine. See Leviticus 19:23; 20:2; 25:10, 18; 26:32, and so forth. As the Gentile nations were not given tithing laws and Levites were not instructed to go to the Gentiles and take tithe from them, the term **"the land"** in Leviticus 27:30 really refers to the land of Israel.

George Foot Moore, in his work on Judaism (one of the recognized authorities on Jewish religion in the time of Christ) had the following to say about the law of the tithe in Leviticus 27: **"All of these applied in the letter of the law only to the land of Israel, however, at any time its boundaries might be defined"** *(Judaism in the First Centuries of the Christian Era,* vol. II, p.71). Moore went on to point out that the land of Babylon was finally accepted as part of the land of Israel—a "tithable" land—because so many Jews were resident in the area. Egypt was finally accepted as a tithable land. In the earlier time of Joseph, however, Egypt

149

but this was only because there was such a huge population of Jews living in that region.

3. Tithing never concerned giving 10% of your income, but was focused on agricultural products and the increase in herds of animals.

4. Only the owners of farms who produced products of agriculture or animal husbandry paid tithes.

5. Numerous other industries (like fishing and mining) are mentioned in the Bible, but tithing was never associated with these.

6. Tithes were only permitted to be given to the Levitical priesthood and to give them to anyone else would have been a sin.

7. It was the tenth animal that passed under the rod which was the tithed animal. In theory, a person could own nine prized animals

---

did not pay tithe as shown by the one-fifth produce which was paid to Pharaoh and the four-fifths that went to the people. The lands east of Jordan came to be acknowledged as tithable: Ammon, Moab and Syria—at least the parts of those lands that David conquered and where many Jews came to live.

Other Gentile lands, on the other hand, such as Asia Minor, Greece or Italy were not allowed as lands which could produce tithe. The produce of those lands was considered as be-ing impure and not holy enough to support the Levitical priesthood in its function at the holy Temple. As Edersheim records, even the very dust of heathen lands was reckoned as defiled (*Life and Times of Jesus the Messiah,* vol. I, p.9). This is why tithe was not acceptable from them.

At any rate, the strict reading of the law demanded that the tithe come only from the land of Israel—which was later interpreted to include those areas east and north of Palestine and Egypt where the populations were predominantly Jewish. All other areas were proscribed. This fact about tithing may be surprising to many Christians, but this is an actual fact that is revealed in the Law of God. Many preachers and evangelists know these facts, but they fail to tell the laity about them simply because they believe the people would not fund their churches if they were privy to these facts. But it is time for all people to know the truth of the biblical revelation. To be guided strictly by the statements of biblical law, it would be improper to pay tithe on products from the United States, Britain, or other Gentile lands. (Ernest L. Martin – The Tithing Dilemma, ASK Publications: Portland: Oregon, 2002)

150

and not be required to tithe because God took the tenth animal, not the first out of ten.

8. It is a very false and evil teaching to say that Christian pastors now have taken over the role of the Levitical Priesthood and are now eligible to accept the tithe and that churches have now taken the place of the Temple in Jerusalem as the only legitimate site in ancient times where tithes were to be designated.

9. It is also totally false to replace the ideas of "you are cursed with a curse," "the tithe", "robbing God" and "the storehouse" found in Malachi 3[35], with the income of modern Christians, ministers working in church buildings and the need to support modern churches today. This is another one of those supposed "clear and plain Biblical teachings" like corporal punishment/spanking/smacking which when researched further we find that it represents a serious error in what Christians are required to do relative to supporting Christ's work on earth at this time.

What is very interesting about the New Testament references to tithing is that you only find a few mentions in the Gospels with Jesus speaking to His people while He was in Israel and among the Israelites and you only find a brief mention of the teaching again in Hebrews 7. There is no other reference in any of Paul's writings nor those of any of the other apostles to tithing. Tithing never appears in the nine letters to the seven churches (Romans to Thessalonians). There is a reason for this. It is because tithing

---

[35] "Will man rob God? Yet you are robbing me. But you say, 'How have we robbed you?' In your tithes and contributions. You are cursed with a curse, for you are robbing me, the whole nation of you. Bring the full tithe into the storehouse, that there may be food in my house. And thereby put me to the test, says the Lord of hosts, if I will not open the windows of heaven for you and pour down for you a blessing until there is no more need." (Malachi 3:8-10 ESV)

had no relevance to Gentile Christians in the past nor does it have any relevance today. Of course, it was still binding on Jewish Christians who were observing the Law of Moses and for those who still lived in the Land of Israel while the Temple was still in existence. This does not mean that worthy Christian activities should not be supported generously, but not with the Biblical tithe because tithing is a teaching linked only to the economy of the Holy Temple and the land of Israel.

Unfortunately, most of the advocates of tithing will never point any of these issues out. They will just wrongly focus in on Malachi 3 and home in on Jesus' teachings where He mentioned tithing and St. Paul's references in Hebrews 7. More unfortunately they never mention that these teachings were directed to believers in Judaism and those Jewish Christians who remained observant in the Law of Moses, retained circumcision, wore phylacteries, kept the Sabbath and Holy Days, clean food laws, physical purity laws and all of the 613 Laws of Moses in the land of Israel.

In conclusion, tithing is a teaching just for the Land of Israel and is focused on the Temple system. Any other interpretation about tithing is, in my view, a false teaching of man and is not relevant for Christians today. It is essential that Christians today free themselves from these false teachings which seek to extract a few scriptures from the book of Hebrews in particular out of context which are used to enslave people in a type of imprisonment theology which includes corporal punishment.

What these evidences point to is strongly supplementing an already very strong case presented in the previous quotes showing to whom the book of Hebrews was written. We assert here that it was written to Jewish believers in our Lord Jesus focusing on Jerusalem and the country surrounding that city.

Further links between tithing and corporal punishment/spanking/smacking

One might find it hard on the surface that there is a connection between the subjects of Tithing and that of Corporal Punishment/Spanking/Smacking, but there is definitely a connection between these two subjects. The connection is found due to the fact that, unfortunately, today many Christian pastors use the same mistaken methodology to say that tithing and corporal punishment/spanking/smacking are relevant today.

These errors start in the Hebrew Bible (the Old Testament) in both cases. For tithing, the teaching begins for Christians today not in the New Testament, but in the book of Malachi. For corporal punishment/spanking/smacking, we can say exactly the same thing, but instead of the book of Malachi, the teaching begins in the book of Proverbs.

In both cases, the texts in Proverbs around corporal punishment/spanking/smacking are misinterpreted as are those texts in the book of Malachi surrounding tithing.

I would urge anyone interested for further study on these important subjects to refer first to my first book on corporal punishment/spanking/smacking referenced earlier in this book and available for free on my website (www.biblechild.com) as well as the links to my late father's work on tithing given earlier.

The following chart can give us some further information on this subject:

Subject	Texts from the Old Testament	Texts from the New Testament	Mentioned by Paul in any letters to the seven Gentile Churches?	Mentioned by Paul in the book of Hebrews?
Tithing	Leviticus 27:30-34 Malachi 3:8-11	Matt. 23:23; Luke 11:42 Heb. 7:4-9	No	Yes, mentioned briefly. (Heb. 7)
-Corporal Punishment -Spanking -Smacking	Proverbs 10:13, 13:23,24; 19:18; 22:15; 23:13,14; 29:15	Hebrews 12:5-11	No	Yes, mentioned in a way that many Christians today say supports the idea. (Heb. 12)

When we review the above chart, we can see some similarities in how these two doctrines have been constructed and on what bases. They both rely heavily on Old Testament texts, which are adapted in some ways attempting to demonstrate the universality of these principles and are then supplemented with additional references in the New Testament. However, the important things to notice are that in both cases, the teachings rely on the book of Hebrews and more importantly, there are NO references to these teachings in any of the nine letters sent to the seven churches of St. Paul, which represent the teachings given to those believers in Jesus who came to faith outside of a stream dominated by the principles of the Hebrew Bible. When we study these two matters more carefully, we find they are both constructed doctrinally in the same mistaken way and are both misapplied today to Christian believers.

APPENDIX II

The Amanuenses in Scripture and the Book of Hebrews

In this book, it has been asserted that St. Paul is the author of the book of Hebrews. Numerous ancient testimonies have been presented from the Eastern and Western branches of the early church attesting to this fact. I know that this view is considered a minority view today among New Testament scholars.

The majority of scholars do not accept that St. Paul wrote Hebrews or some of the other books that we normally associate with him. Professors Cross and Livingstone provide a general survey of the evidence concerning this point:

"Traditionally included among the letters of St. Paul, this Epistle unlike most other in the New Testament, does not contain the name of the writer or that of those addressed."[36]

As noted earlier in this book, St. Paul did not identify himself openly as the author. Because of this (among other reasons), most modern

---

[36] Cross, F.L. and Livingstone, E.A, The Oxford Dictionary of the Christian Church: Oxford University Press; Oxford: UK, 1983. p.625

scholars believe that someone else wrote this book. Professors Cross and Livingstone give the general summary of this view saying:

"From an early date the Epistle was received at Alexandria as Pauline, whether considered as a translation by St. Luke from St. Paul's Hebrew (Clement of Alexandria, ap. Eusebius, H.E., vi. 14), or as St. Paul's in substance, but committed to writing by someone else. (Origen ap. Eusebius, H.E. vi. 24), while in the East, generally, e.g. by the Council of Antioch (264) and the later Eastern Fathers, it was regularly quoted as St. Paul's own composition."

Professors Cross and Livingstone also point out that:

"Modern scholars, however, almost unanimously consider that that internal evidence marks it as non-Pauline, while its style shows that it is unlikely to be a translation. Clearly both the author and his intended readers were thoroughly familiar with Jewish worship and the latter were probably converts from Judaism. ... We learn that the author was a contemporary of Timothy (13:21), temporarily absent from those whom he was addressing and expecting to return to them (13:19). His identification with, e.g. **Barnabas** (Tertullian and certain modern scholars), **Apollos** (Martin Luther, C. Spicq, and H.W. Montefiore), **Aquila** (H. Alford and others), or **Priscilla** (A. Harnack) cannot be more than conjectures." (*ibid.* pg. 626)

It should come as no surprise to us (who have been taught the old standard line about the 30 men who wrote the Bible) that not every word purported to appear in a certain book was written by the original author whose name may appear on the book.

A very simple example of this concerns the death of Moses, which is referenced in a narrative text found in Deuteronomy 34:5-12. While this text is certainly a part of the Mosaic body of literature, which we call 'the Law of Moses" or 'the Torah', it is clear that this text was added by some type of an authorized secretarial figure. This is just one place where we find this phenomenon happening.

In fact, not only are small explanatory texts added or placed in collections of books written by others, but whole books which bear the names of certain persons, were in fact written by other people, known as *"amanuenses"*, an academic word for a *secretary*.'

Most of the New Testament books were *not* directly written by the people whose names appear on them. We have referred to this earlier in this book.

"As for the Gospel of Mark, it has long been known that John Mark was recognized as the **secretary**, or **amanuensis**, of the apostle Peter. Indeed, in the Gospel of Mark the great humility of Peter is conspicuous in all parts of it. Where anything is related which might show Peter's weakness, we find it recorded in detail whereas the other Gospels often show Peter's strengths. In Mark there is scarcely an action by Christ in which Peter is not mentioned as being a close observer or communicant. All of this affords a reasonable deduction that the writer of the Gospel of Mark was an eyewitness and close observer of the events recorded about Christ's life from the baptism of John to his crucifixion in Jerusalem. The ancient testimony of Papias, in the early second century, that Mark was the **secretary** of the apostle Peter (and not the actual eyewitness himself) has such good credentials, and the internal evidence of the Gospel itself is

157

so compatible to this view that it seems evident that the **Gospel of Mark** is really the **Gospel of Peter.**"[37]

"There was no reason for such a change because it can be shown that Mark and Luke were simply the secretaries for two apostles: Peter and Paul. **It was common in the first century for men of authority to have amanuenses (official secretaries) to write their letters or books for them.** Paul used such people on many occasions. His writing of the Book of Romans is an example. **"I Tertius, who wrote this epistle,** salute you in the Lord"** (Romans 16:22). **Most, if not all, of Paul's epistles were actually written by amanuenses whom he maintained on his staff of transcribers.** Since Luke was a companion of Paul, it is perfectly proper to assume that Luke's Gospel and the Book of Acts were actually the historical record which **Paul** called **"my Gospel"** in Second Timothy 2:8." (*ibid*. pg.335)

Therefore, it becomes quite easy to explain why the Greek language or style of Hebrews might be quite different than some of St. Paul's other writings. It was probably written down by someone else, but fundamentally the writing was inspired by the pen of St. Paul overall. Couple this with the fact that in the majority of ancient manuscripts, we find the book of Hebrews positioned after the book of II Thessalonians and before 1st Timothy in the original order of the New Testament.

---

[37] Martin, E. L. Restoring the Original Bible: ASK Publications; Portland: OR, 1994. p.335-6

About the Author

Samuel Martin was born in England and is the youngest child of Dr. Ernest L. and Helen R. Martin, who are both Americans. He lived in the UK for the first seven years of his life before moving to the USA with his family. He lived in the USA until 2001 when he married a native Israeli and relocated to live in Jerusalem.

He and his wife, Sonia, have two daughters, Jessica and Christine.

His experience with biblical scholarship began at an early age. His father lead a program in conjunction with Hebrew University and the late Professor Benjamin Mazar, where over a five year period, some 450 college students came to work on an archaeological excavation in Jerusalem starting in 1969.

Since that first trip, Samuel has visited Israel on 14 different occasions living more than 19 years of his life in the country. He has toured all areas of Israel as well as worked in several archaeological excavations.

He writes regularly on biblical subjects with a particular interest in children, families, nature, science, the Bible, and gender in the Biblical context.

Website: www.biblechild.com
Contact: info@biblechild.com
Facebook: https://www.facebook.com/byblechyld/
Blog: www.samuelmartin.blogspot.com
Amazon: https://www.amazon.com/Samuel-Martin

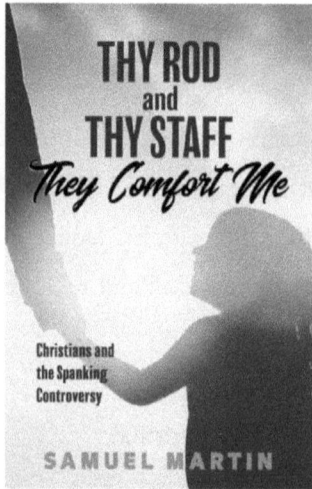

THY ROD
and
THY STAFF
They Comfort Me

Christians and
the Spanking
Controversy

SAMUEL MARTIN

The first book in the series

There are few Biblical subjects where more misunderstanding exists among Christians and child rights advocates today than that of spanking children.

"Thy Rod and Thy Staff, They Comfort Me: Christians and the Spanking Controversy," seeks to increase the level of understanding about this issue by exploring these questions:

- Does the Bible teach that spanking a child will save him from Hell?

- Does the Bible teach that spanking a child should bring tears?

- In Bible times, what age were the texts concerning spanking children found in Proverbs applied to?

- What did some of the most respected Christian theologians of our time including Dr. Karl Barth and Rev. Dwight Moody think about spanking children?

- Are the main Christian advocates for spanking children trained Christian theologians teaching in universities, or are they conservative fundamentalist Christian pastors, Christian politicians, Christian psychologists, lay church members and Christian school leaders, and what difference does this make?

- Are there doctrines surrounding spanking children which are not found in the Bible at all?

- Are Children's Rights activists, who are not trained Bible scholars, justified in attacking the Bible?

- What do conservative Jewish Rabbis, who have the Old Testament as their Holy Scriptures, think about spanking children today?

FEATURES OF THIS VOLUME

- 353 Separate Biblical texts referenced
- 82 Separate references fro Hebrew and Christian scholars
- 39 Authoritative Biblical reference works utilized
- Key new information revealed from an early Egyptian text which is also found today in the Biblical book of Proverbs concerning spanking

"*Thy Rod and Thy Staff, They Comfort Me: Christians and the Spanking Controversy,*" (published in 2006) was not sold, but has been available as a free download on numerous sites on the web and through www.biblechild.com. A printed version is now also available for purchase through Amazon.

www.ingramcontent.com/pod-product-compliance
Lightning Source LLC
Chambersburg PA
CBHW022009090410

42741CB00007B/962